LOST
HOLLYWOOD

LA
WEEKLY
BOOKS

An LA Weekly Book
for St. Martin's Press

New York

LOST
HOLLYWOOD

DAVID WALLACE

Title page caption: In Hollywood's golden age, premieres like this at the long-gone Fox Carthay Circle near Beverly Hills were the last word in glamour and excitement.

All photographs courtesy of Bison Archives

LA Weekly Books is a trademark of LA Weekly Media, Inc.

www.stmartins.com

Book design by James Sinclair

Library of Congress Cataloging-in-Publication Data
Wallace, David.
        Lost Hollywood / David Wallace.—1st ed.
            p.   cm.
        ISBN 0-312-26195-0
        1. Motion picture actors and actresses—Homes and haunts—California—Los Angeles.   2. Motion picture industry—California—Los Angeles—History.   I. Title.
        PN1993.5.U65 W29 2001
        684'.8'097949409041—dc21   00-045968

First Edition: April 2001

10 9 8 7 6 5 4 3 2 1

For my son Christopher

Contents

Foreword

The generic "thing" we think of as Hollywood likes to destroy and bury its past. Most traces of the original la-la-land are dead, buried, and gone. But now the maestro of entertainment history, David Wallace, has unearthed real treasures. Archaeology is a passion of mine. And so are the movies: the history of the movies, the making of movies, and the stars we have all known, loved, or hated. This book combines both of my passions, examining the priceless and fascinating past of Hollywoodland.

Hollywoodland was the original lettering of the famous sign that hovers, iconlike above the Hollywood Hills. Today it exists simply as "Hollywood," but what a tale Wallace has to tell of how this great symbol fell into disrepair and was almost obliterated altogether.

Here we get the foibles, follies, houses, yachts, cars, studios, and restaurants of the glorious and glamorous yesterdays when stars *really* caught the public's imagination. This was America's beginning love affair with the cult of celebrity. These were the early silent years when flicks were the opium of the masses and audiences believed every word written in *Photoplay* and *Modern Screen*. There was the invention of sound and every other technical achievement one could dream of. But chiefly there were stars and star makers.

Can you think of anyone famous today who would lure ten thousand people to a funeral? Princess Diana comes to mind, but in the early screen days William Desmond Taylor lured them because he had been murdered. The silent-screen beauty Mary Miles Minter was implicated in this still unsolved death, and she fainted at his funeral. *Lost Hollywood* is crammed with such stories.

This work is delicious. It tells us that Geraldine Farrar had a contract clause assuring her of two dollars per minute of daylight she spent in California. She also got a railroad car, a mansion, a bungalow on the set, expenses for her current lover, and flowers thrown at her during every public appearance.

Where else but here, in this book, will we discover that the two tablets of "The Ten Commandments," used in Cecil B. DeMille's last film, were attached to the wall of the little St. Stephen's Episcopal Church of Hollywood for the great director's funeral? They had been hewn out of the red granite of Mount Sinai and were enscribed in early Bronze Age Canaanite lettering.

David Wallace has given the truly star-struck an indescribable gift. He has found Lost Hollywood.

—Liz Smith

Acknowledgments

This book is largely due to the enthusiastic support of Adolfo Nodal, Loretta Barrett, Nicholas Mullendore, Elizabeth Beier, Michael Connor, Marc Wanamaker, Dale` Olson, Paul Jasmin, Bob and Donna Morris Grumbles, Peter Bloedt, and to the ever-lively ghosts of Hollywood.

LOST
HOLLYWOOD

It used to be called the Los Angeles Metropolitan Airport: it's the Van Nuys Airport, a popular private aviation facility. In 1942, its entrance was transformed into that of *Casablanca*'s Aéro-Gare (complete with era-appropriate license plates and Air France emblems), where early in the film Conrad Veidt, playing the Nazi Colonel Strasser, disembarks. Airport shots later in the movie were made in the studio or with miniatures.

Introduction

Ghosts exist.

In film, images (ghosts) of people we love or hate do the things we fantasize about or recoil from in stories and settings equally phantasmal.

The ghosts of Hollywood embody and animate our collective and individual consciences, our ethics, our relationships, our dreams, and our darkest sides. The stories that flicker on the silver screen, and the people who bring them to life—the actors, producers, directors, crews, and publicists—have shaped the way we live. It has been said that the real challenge for a storyteller in relating a pre-Christian tale is to remove Christian values from the characters' motivations and actions. I believe that for a storyteller a few centuries down the way, it will be even harder to remove values of the movie era from today's civilization. Film, in its century, has changed civilization as profoundly as Christianity shaped Western culture in the previous nineteen centuries.

Art, architecture, fashion, design, literature, music, dance, social behaviors—even religion itself—have all been consumed by film and changed. Gods and goddesses far more dynamic and powerful than any in ancient mythology have been raised up and cast down. Has there ever been anyone more idolized—in all meanings of the word—than Greta Garbo, or Douglas Fairbanks, or Marilyn Monroe (add martyrdom), or James Dean (martyrdom again), or Charlie Chaplin, or Tom Cruise, or name your favorite?

Or consider the monuments of civilization. The Romans may be best remembered by the Coliseum, the Egyptians for the pyramids, and the ancient Chinese by their Great Wall. Each is real, each has substance, each you can walk up to and touch. But to future generations the most popular image of the American South in the mid–nineteenth century may well be *Gone With the Wind*'s plantation house, itself quickly gone with the wind as soon as filming was completed. And far more than Winthrop Rockefeller's castle Biltmore or William Randolph Hearst's San Simeon, the image of America's plutocracy is that of Xanadu, the make-believe San Simeon of Orson Welles's *Citizen Kane*. And which is more real, the airport in the opening scenes of *Casablanca* or the Van Nuys Airport in the San Fernando Valley (today a private aviation facility but once grandiosely named the Los Angeles Metropolitan Airport)? They're one and the same, but which is more *real*? And which is the ghost?

As film has shaped our culture, so too it has shaped a small town called Hollywood. In the beginning, Hollywood wasn't the most important center of filmmaking, Europe was. But fairly quickly, a world war and entre-preneurial moxie changed all that, and the film and entertainment business hasn't been the same since. Physically and metaphorically, as the industry expanded beyond the town's limits to handle the evolution of the silent era to sound, to television, and to today's dot-com world, Hollywood became and remained synonymous with entertainment.

Like any cultural phenomenon, the entertainment business has a huge downside. Movie stars—whose sole claim to fame is frequently no more than a physical beauty exploited to feed the public's dream-fulfillment fantasies—are raised to totemic levels. Historical fact is more often than not altered to provide a good story. Superficiality reigns, lust is fulfilled, talent exploited and ruthlessly discarded, and ethics and morals are trivialized. And why? The bottom line in Holly-wood is and always has been money.

Genius too has been debased. In Mozart's time, and even in the early part of this century, humankind acknowledged only two or three authentic geniuses a century. In Hollywood, Charlie Chaplin unques-tionably qualified, but now the very term has become meaningless as nearly every successful new talent is hyped by the PR industry as a genius, though no more (and probably far less) talented than Marlene Dietrich, Gloria Swanson, Cary Grant, or Gregory Peck.

But there is an upside. And a big one. One far more important and far-reaching than the image being sold of the industry's latest fifteen-minute wonder.

Claims are constantly made these days about the Americanization of the world by the Internet, but that globalization really began with film itself (particularly silent film), which brought sagas of the Old West and brittle, sophisticated urban comedies to people who had never seen a light bulb, let alone an airplane. And judging from the continuing box office (and television) figures, the impact of American films on the world's civilizations isn't going to lessen any time soon. It is estimated that in Hollywood alone, the business generates twenty-three billion dollars annually. Worldwide gross revenues and secondary income from the entertainment industry account for between 5 and 10 percent of the U.S. gross national product, according to some experts. That, folks, is upward of a half a *trillion* dollars.

Hollywood's monuments may be physical (like the Garden of Allah, once filmdom's most famous and most notorious hotel), or they may be less tangible, like the old contract system—Hollywood's version of slavery—or the way movies were made in the silent era, so different from today.

We're going to revisit that world in *Lost Hollywood*, with its hopes, dreams, triumphs and tragedies, laughter and tears, and the values that made it live. That includes an entire era when Los Angeles, often dismissed today as "la-la-land," was the intellectual capital of America.

We're going to revisit the monuments that Hollywood erected to that long-gone life too, monuments like the Hollywood Bowl and the Hollywood sign, which the world instantly associates with the film capital but which have changed radically from their early years. And we're going to visit the homey aspects of that long-lost era, places like Schwab's drugstore, where Lana Turner *wasn't* discovered, and publisher William Randolph Hearst's Ocean House where Charlie Chaplin, Harold Lloyd, and even Winston Churchill once cavorted by the sea.

Ghosts live.

It's 1917, and the legendary Mack Sennett is directing ZaSu
Pitts in her first movie, *The Little Princess*. Pitts, who began
her career as a film heroine (she costarred in D. W. Griffith's *Greed* in 1923), would become better known as a
comedienne in such films as *Mrs. Wiggs of the Cabbage
Patch* (1934) and *Life With Father* (1947). Pitts also costarred in the *Oh Susanna* television series from 1956 to
1959, successfully moving from silent to sound films to
television in a forty-two-year career.

In the Beginning . . .

It was all an accident; Hollywood, that is. The town that would become so proficient at creating fake accidents to amuse, fascinate, or terrify a future audience numbering in the billions was itself a serendipitous product of the right timing and the right location. It was neither a transportation nexus like the river town of Pittsburgh nor a harbor city like San Francisco (or Hollywood's neighbor, the Los Angeles harbor city of San Pedro) nor a railroad town like Omaha or even nearby San Bernardino. In the beginning, it was nothing.

Nothing, that is, except a place of gentle hills rolling southward below a number of canyons that carried winter runoff from the slopes of the yet-to-be named Santa Monica Mountains near a wide pass that led to the also unnamed San Fernando Valley.

In August 1767, Gaspar de Portolá's expedition from Mexico to Monterey, the capital of Spanish California, camped near the site of today's Dodger Field in Elysian Park. There they discovered a number of brush-hut villages populated by a tribe of Indians; the largest was at the north end of today's Sycamore Avenue. The explorers named them the Gabrilinos, after the Mission of San Gabriel Archangel located in the then far reaches of the San Fernando Valley and responsible for the spiritual life of the area's native population. The Indians have long since vanished, leaving only their name for their homeland, *Cahuengna*, which apparently meant "little hills." Simplified by the Spanish to Cahuenga, it is now the name of a major Hollywood street and the pass through which commuters whiz (or curse during rush hour gridlock) on the Hollywood Freeway.

In the 1870s, a toll station and inn was built by Cahuenga Pass on the overland mail route to Northern California that wended its way through the San Fernando Valley, then a waterless, chaparral- and sagebrush-covered desert. Kit Carson, whose life would be limned several times in movies later made nearby, was one of the carriers. At the north end of the pass, where Universal City is located today, the commander of the Mexican forces in California surrendered in 1847, enabling California to become a territory of the United States the following year.

As significant as the state's future statehood was the discovery of oil a generation later on the Spanish land grant that occupied most of the west side of Hollywood's present site. Named the Rancho la Brea for the tar (*brea*) that seeped to the surface, it made many early settlers very rich, among them one Arthur Gilmore, whose dairy farm would soon sprout hundreds of oil derricks and one day become the site of CBS's Television City and a famous farmer's market. Another land grant was the Rancho las Feliz, which would become Hollywood's Griffith Park after being deeded to the city in 1898. By the 1880s, most of what was being called the Cahuenga Valley was filled by 160-acre hay, grain, vegetable, and fruit farms situated in what was billed as the Frostless Belt. One early settler, George Caralambo, even brought along a herd of camels, originally bought in Turkey to open a government caravan route between army posts in California and New Mexico. After the Civil War, the plan was abandoned, and the camels were turned loose where Hollywood is today. By the turn of the century, all of them had disappeared.

Then in 1883, Harvey Wilcox, a Prohibitionist from Topeka, Kansas, and his wife, Daeida, arrived and started buying land stretching as far west as the future site of UCLA to be developed for homes. His choice for his own home was a spot near Cahuenga Pass filled with fig and apricot trees. He discovered it when he and his wife, in their carriage drawn by two prize Arabian horses brought from Kansas, pulled off the dirt road leading up the pass for a rest during a Sunday excursion.

Wilcox bought 160 acres and promptly began to develop them as the site of a Protestant Christian temperance community. The next year, while traveling east on vacation, Daeida met a woman on the train who mentioned that she had named her summer home in Ohio Hollywood. Daeida loved the name and on her return gave it to their new development. (She also planted two holly bushes, which, it is said, didn't do too well.) The name Hollywood first appeared officially on Wilcox's meticulously drawn map of the subdivision, filed with the county recorder on February 1, 1887. Within three years, real estate prices, originally $150 an acre, had tripled.

By 1900, the community had a hotel, two markets, a school, two churches, a newspaper, a post office, and a population of five hundred living on wide dirt avenues shaded by pepper trees whose fruit was as big as dates. Los Angeles, with a population of close to a hundred thousand, lay only seven miles to the east through hills of citrus trees; it was an easy and picturesque commute on a streetcar of the new Pacific Railroad, which ran down the middle of Prospect Avenue, later Hollywood Boulevard. Two years later Hollywood became a city. Among the ordinances was one prohibiting the sale of liquor except by pharmacists and outlawing the driving of cattle through the streets in herds of more than two hundred.

Filmmaking arrived in 1911 with the coming of the Nestor Film Company from New Jersey. Within a year, more than a dozen other film companies had joined it, drawn by the climate, which permitted shooting for more than three hundred days a year, as well as by the variety of scenery and cheap labor costs

Mack Sennett settled in Edendale near present-day Glendale in 1912, and a group of early producers—among them Carl Laemmle of Universal and Jesse Lasky and Cecil B. DeMille's company (later merged with Adolph Zukor's Famous Players Company)—settled in the heart of Hollywood near the intersection of Sunset Boulevard and Vine Street. For more than a decade, however, everything remained fairly primitive. Studios, so grand by the 1930s, were little more than a stage with four posts holding up canvas to diffuse the sun. There was no electricity: The sun supplied the light for making movies. In fact, there was little more than a tremendous sense of optimism, and the early filmmakers needed all of it they could summon. There was a problem far more serious for early independent filmmakers than the weather, and although the move to California provided a stopgap solution, it would plague them for years to come.

Thomas Edison claimed he invented the motion picture process in 1889, although the work of William Friese-Greene in Britain almost certainly predated Edison's. Nevertheless, Edison certainly knew how to market it, demonstrating an early projector called the Vitascope in New York City in 1896 while the inventor, one Thomas Armat, stood by.

As shrewd as Edison was, however, he failed to register his Kinetoscope patents in Europe, where manufacturers began turning out first-class motion picture equipment without fear of reprisals. To protect his patents (which covered the sprocket holes since there was no way he could patent the film itself, made by Eastman), Edison, in partnership with his former rival Biograph, formed the Motion Picture Patents Company (known as the Trust) in 1908, which licensed equipment manufactured under the Edison patents to friendly producers. Nestor, then doing business in Bayonne, New Jersey, under its original name, Centaur Film Company, was not one of them.

As movies—then called flickers—burgeoned in popularity, scores of new companies got into the business, which was becoming, as film historian Kevin Brownlow writes, "as tough and dangerous as any gold rush." For years, the Trust sued any company that dared to make or import non-Edison cameras and projection equipment, forcing them to flee the New York–New Jersey areas where the film industry was born for distant locations like Florida, Cuba, and eventually California. The Trust's common way of putting the competition out of business was to have hired gunmen shoot holes in their cameras. If they missed the cameras and hit the cameraman . . . well, too bad. It was war.

Ironically, it is the pirates whose names we remember today, people like Carl Laemmle (who formed Universal Pictures, absorbed Nestor in 1912, and then behaved about as imperiously as the Trust itself), Cecil B. DeMille, Samuel Goldwyn, and D. W. Griffith. Despite the three thousand miles and five day's travel time separating them from the East, they had to be constantly on guard after the Trust people started infiltrating Hollywood to sabotage the filmmaker's equipment—at least until the government ordered the Trust to disband after its monopoly was successfully prosecuted under the Sherman Act. DeMille, for example, received numerous anonymous threats to his life and was shot at twice in his first months in Hollywood. The director was certain it was the Trust trying to kill him, but the perpetrators were never caught. On more than one occasion, he slept in his first studio armed with a shotgun to guard his film. Like many other early filmmakers, he carried a .45 revolver conspicuously in a holster on his belt. Eventually he owned eighty-six guns, often using them as props for his movies.

"World War One was the reason for Hollywood," author Anita Loos once recalled. "At the time war broke out, movies had gained a very substantial place in Europe, and in Italy they were particularly good, and there was no need for Hollywood [and, Loos might have added, no Trust to strangle creativity]. But the war broke out, and that changed the whole scene. . . ."

She wasn't entirely correct. American films had been gaining on their European rivals before the war. But there is no question that the conflict offered the option of making highly profitable antiwar (later anti-German) films, eventually requiring an order from Washington to tone it all down.

Hollywood, however, was on its way, and nothing would stop it.

Shooting movies in the early days was a seat-of-the-pants effort. No one knows the name of this film being made around 1914 on a ramshackle stage near the intersection of Gower Street and Sunset Boulevard, nor who the actors, director, and cameraman were (most were anonymous then). Most films made at the time shared several common characteristics: For enough light to expose the slow film, they were shot open to the sky (the sun was occasionally muted by drawing muslin curtains as seen in the background); they were short (average length eighteen minutes); and they were made in two or three days to satisfy the appetite of a movie-mad public.

2 Gower Gulch——Hollywood's Ground Zero

In 1869, a farmer named John T. Gower migrated to California from Hawaii, bought one of the 160-acre pieces of land being sold in what is now Hollywood, and planted wheat and barley. Today the intersection of Sunset Boulevard and the street named in Gower's memory are bracketed by industry restaurant hangouts, Pinot Hollywood and a Denny's. But when Hollywood was in its infancy, the corner of Sunset Boulevard and Gower Street was ground zero for everything that would eventually grow, for better or for worse, into the single most important molder of contemporary civilization's popular culture: the world's greatest film and television industry.

Far more than wars, famines, financial booms and busts, and natural, social, and technological disasters, Hollywood's treatment of humanity's traditions, triumphs, tragedies, hero's, villains, religions, and legends—usually transformed into myth—would shape, and continues to shape, how we live and what we believe. It was, and is, the stage set of our collective consciousness.

The first Hollywood stage set was built exactly on this spot, at the northwest corner of the then dusty, unpaved intersection (long buried under a foot of pavement) in 1911, and the first movie made on it was producers William and David Horseley's *The Law of the Range*. Their studio was called the Nestor Studio, and it moved into Blondeau's Tavern, the village's first hotel, in October of that year. The pair paid thirty dollars a month for the property, including a barn used for props, a corral for the horses appearing in Westerns (formerly for guests' horses), and several smaller buildings, including a bungalow used for offices. Nestor quickly established an approach to film production that would rule the industry for years: Churn 'em out fast. Two or more one- and two-reelers were shot at a time (their forty-foot-square stage had a different background on each end) based on scripts usually written the night before. Incidentally, *The Law of the Range* was not the first movie made in California; that honor went to *The Heart of a Race Tout*, filmed in 1909 by the Selig Polyscope Company on an outdoor stage adjoining a vacant Chinese laundry, which served as dressing rooms and offices, at Eighth and Olive Streets in downtown Los Angeles.

Within months, the intersection of Gower and Sunset became the true center of working Hollywood. So many small, struggling film companies were built along Gower that it was dubbed "Poverty Row" or, a little more politely, "Gower Gulch." During the teens and early 1920s, dozens of these small storefront studios, with names like Sterling, Quality, Waldorf, and, more appropriately, Goodwill Studios, barely existed, tottering on the brink of bankruptcy by churning out one- and two-reel films.

It wasn't much better for wishful movie stars either. So many extras used to hang around the intersection hoping for a day's work that, in 1921, the Hollywood Chamber of Commerce began taking out advertisements to discourage them. One, echoing the employment dynamic that has existed in the film industry for nearly a century, read, "Out of 100,000 Persons Who Started at the Bottom of the Screen's Ladder of Fame, only FIVE Reached the Top."

The origin of the name Gower Gulch has been the subject of much speculation over the years. Some have said that the high walls of the sound stages along Gower south of Sunset created the feeling of a gulch. Others have claimed that the name arose because so many Westerns were made in and around the area. There is a little-known fact, however, which I believe reveals the true origin of the name. Four blocks above Sunset Boulevard there is a paved alleyway behind the small Episcopal Church of Saint Stephen's (which Cecil B. DeMille and his family once attended). According to church records, before the alley was paved over it was the site of an open ditch carrying runoff from the hills above Hollywood. Since the ditch paralleled Gower Street, and given the film community's penchant for hyperbole, it was only natural that it would rather grandiosely be called Gower Gulch.

Whatever the origin of the nickname, Gower Gulch's close accessibility to all sorts of locations certainly enhanced its popularity among early filmmakers. ("A rock is a rock and a tree is a tree," one early producer said. "Shoot it in Griffith Park.")

In 1926, Harry Cohn and his brother Jack located their fledgling CBC Studio at the intersection and quickly changed the name to Columbia Pictures (they were afraid that CBC, the initials of the founding partners, suggested an acronym for "corned beef and cabbage"). The soundstages are still there, now leased for various indoor sports activities. On the Gower Street sides of those soundstages, twenty- by thirty-foot frames once showcased billboards advertising the studio's latest productions. Unlike similar billboards at working studios (including today's Columbia Pictures, now located in Burbank), these remained empty for years before their removal. Once they trumpeted the release of such immortal Columbia productions as *It Happened One Night* (1934), director Frank Capra's Oscar-winning evergreen romantic comedy starring Clark Gable and Claudette Colbert. The picture and Gable were so popular at the time that when he took off his shirt revealing he was not wearing an undershirt, sales of that then-essential article of men's apparel plummeted. In 1937, it was the announcement of another Capra film, the utopian *Lost Horizon*, that filled those billboards.

Down Gower at Melrose Avenue, similar billboards on the soundstages of RKO proclaimed the release in 1932 of *King Kong* and, two years later, Ginger Rogers and Fred Astaire's classic *The Gay Divorcee*. RKO moved into the television age when Lucille Ball and her husband,

Desi Arnaz, took over the studio for their Desilu Productions. Now it's part of Paramount.

A mile or so west of Gower on Santa Monica Boulevard was one of the most famous of Hollywood's early studios, the huge (for the time) complex erected in 1922 on the site of the Jesse B. Hampden studio by America's most famous couple, Douglas Fairbanks and Mary Pickford. Later expanded, it became United Artists, the company founded by Doug and Mary (with Charlie Chaplin and D. W. Griffith) to control distribution of their films. Then it became Samuel Goldwyn Studios (with control still held by Pickford until 1955). Now it's a branch of Warner Brothers, itself headquartered in Burbank in the San Fernando Valley. In 1919, Chaplin built his own Tudor-faced studio near the intersection of Sunset and La Brea; later owned by Francis Ford Coppola's Zoetrope Productions, it still stands as the headquarters of Jim Henson Productions.

Just to the east of the intersection of Gower and Sunset is the neocolonial headquarters of Los Angeles's independent television station, KTLA. Of all the studios in the area it probably has the greatest claim to fame. Once belonging to Warner Brothers, this is the place where *The Jazz Singer*, the first successful sound picture, was made in 1927. The huge studio of 20th Century-Fox was once located just a little farther east, at the intersection of Sunset and Western Avenue. In the mid-1930s, after Fox moved everything to its back lot in West Los Angeles (much of which was subsequently developed as today's high-profile shopping and office community known as Century City), the site was used for Spanish-language films and shorts. The original location is now occupied in part by an equally huge discount food market.

Orbiting the intersection of Sunset and Gower were countless satellite industries, among them costumers, film laboratories, camera and lens rental companies, and prop houses as well as the media that covered the industry: *Daily Variety* and the *Hollywood Reporter*. Many of them remain, as well as the radio and television stations that later moved in to take advantage of all the technical support in the area (and brought along some unmatched 1930s streamlined architecture, perhaps best epitomized by the CBS studio at Sunset Boulevard and El Centro Street.

Weather was one of the main reasons for filmmaking's move from the New York area to Hollywood. The sun was the energy source that powered the movies of the time, and without it you couldn't make movies. For years, even interiors were shot outdoors, the sets' ceilings open to the sky. Lights were imperative in the East, and after several false starts the solution was found in the so-called klieg lights (named for the brothers Kliegl, who invented them earlier for theatrical lighting).

Klieg lights were a big improvement over the mercury vapor lights that preceded them. James Morrison, a New York Vitagraph player, once recalled: "We had to wear a blue shirt if we wanted it to photograph white. Real white was too glaring [exactly the same problem would be faced for years by early black-and-white television]. All our dress clothes had to be dyed—even our tan would take white. Klieg lights were coming in, but they used them without any protective glass. The arc throws off a burning carbon dust for several feet around. It gets into your eyes, and they swell up and go pink—this was called klieg eyes. [Actually it was found that klieg eyes were not caused by arc dust, the residue of the burning of the electric arcs in the lights, but by the invisible ultraviolet rays they emitted.] It would take two or three days before they'd be normal. It was agony. Out on the coast, they had constant sunlight, so it was some time before they started using artificial light."

Kliegs arrived in Hollywood soon enough, though (the slow, slow speed of the film available often demanded them even when shooting outdoors), and the problems remained. Opera diva Geraldine Farrar, who made four films for DeMille beginning in 1915 (the most famous being her silent version of Bizet's opera *Carmen* and a saga of Joan of Arc called *Joan the Woman*) and three for Goldwyn, had a terrible but not unusual experience with the klieg lights. "The worst part," she wrote, "was the dreadful white makeup. It was terribly hot and the klieg lights made it worse. In no time the makeup was streaming down your face and back you had to go to make it all up again."

Their unreliability was a problem too. "The kliegs were a great nuisance," Farrar continued. "You'd make the most inspired gesture, and the arc would sputter, the light on your face would flicker, and the shot would be ruined."

The film caused other problems. "My blue eyes photographed

blank," Farrar—like many other actors—complained. The reason: Orthochromatic film, which would be used until panchromatic film came into use in the mid-1920s, wasn't sensitive to blue. "I was horrified at the first day's rushes," wrote Farrar of one experience, "but he [De-Mille] solved the problem. A man held up a black velvet strip. When I stared at it my eyes dilated (and thus the pupils, at any rate, were visible). He was a genius at solving that sort of problem."

DeMille and other directors and cameramen needed to be geniuses. Although the orthochromatic film was fairly sharp in resolving images, its low sensitivity to light demanded extreme accuracy in focus and exposure. Focus was easy; exposure, in an era before the photoelectric cell made exposure meters possible, was based more on previous experience than science. A sign at Universal reminded cameramen of a formula used for generations by many photographers: "If in doubt, shoot at 5.6." If there were unusual circumstances—like photographing in snow or the desert—many cameramen actually carried along their own cumbersome darkroom and developed the film on the spot to see if their exposure was correct.

Although Bell and Howell designed a camera with a motor in it early in the history of filmmaking (the motor was designed to replicate the "official" speed of sixteen frames per second, which was raised to an average of between eighteen and twenty-two frames per second in the mid-1920s; today's 35mm film runs at twenty-four frames per second), it was a long time before the device was accepted. Without a hand crank, how could a cameraman speed up or slow down the action, as was the practice of the time—particularly in slapstick comedy? Or so the thinking went. Projectors with rheostats on the speed regulators brought other problems, as theater managers would frequently speed up the movies to squeeze in extra screenings.

Backlighting, for years one of the most dramatically effective of camera techniques, was an early invention, and like most things in the infant industry it came about by accident. Because Billy Bitzer, D. W. Griffith's cameraman, was as bored as his colleagues with using daylight for dramatic scenes (it was too flat), one day during a lunch break he shot a few feet of Mary Pickford and Owen Moore (her fellow actor and first husband) with the sun *behind* them. The result, creating a halo of Pickford's famed curls, so delighted Griffith that he and Bitzer developed a system of using men carrying mirrors to direct the sun where they wanted it.

Unlike today, all special effects—double exposures, fades, dissolves, and the rest—had to be done inside the camera. It is a fact that all effects used today, including the zoom, traveling shots, matte shots, and the rest of the industry's bag of magic tricks (including Technicolor), although refined and now computerized, were all creations of the film industry's first decades—decades spent within walking distance of Gower Gulch.

Cecil B. DeMille, wearing his trademark boots and holding a megaphone (necessary for directing movies in an era before electronic amplification), is shown here directing his silent 1923 version of *The Ten Commandments* in Guadalupe Sand Dunes near Santa Maria, California. Watching on the right is Jeanie MacPherson, DeMille's longtime scenario writer and trusted confidante. The cameraman is Alvin Wyckoff.

Mr. Movies—Cecil B. DeMille and Filmmaking in Hollywood's Golden Age

It was 1938, and Cecil B. DeMille had just learned that Evelyn Keyes, a young actress making her debut in his film *The Buccaneer*, was dating Anthony Quinn, a twenty-three-year-old Mexican-Irish actor who had played a bit part in the legendary director's *The Plainsman*, made the previous year. "Don't you dare go out with that half-breed again," DeMille reportedly thundered to the terrified Keyes. Only months later, De-Mille's adopted daughter, Katherine, a leading lady in her own right, would marry Quinn. It was one of the very few times in his career that the autocratic DeMille failed to have his way.

In his era, Cecil B. DeMille personified Hollywood and a style of filmmaking now lost forever. Noted for sex comedies in the 1920s, action-adventure films in the 1930s (especially Westerns like *Union Pacific*), and overblown epics in the 1940s and '50s (*The Greatest Show on Earth* and, in 1956, *The Ten Commandments*, his last film) DeMille's movies were often simplistic, jingoistic, and shamelessly sentimental. In the case of his Roman and biblical films, more often than not they were also just plain silly. *Samson and Delilah* (1951), which starred the woefully miscast Hedy Lamarr and Victor Mature, was almost painfully so. Nevertheless, the film was one of DeMille's biggest moneymakers.

DeMille was also a stickler for detail, even when it was wrong-headed, and a rigid disciplinarian on the sets of his seventy films. Now we may laugh over many of his overblown fantasies, but in those simpler times the public loved it all, especially the epics. It is estimated that more than four billion people—then one-and-a-half times the population of the earth—saw a DeMille film in their lifetime. Perhaps it was because he reduced historic characters to neighborly accessibility as they wandered through the kinds of floridly—even vulgarly—grandiose settings that even today are often mistaken for class. (Those settings include lavish bathrooms, which became a DeMille film trademark, apparently motivated by memories of the dark, cramped, cockroach-infested bathroom of his childhood.) In its obituary following DeMille's death from a heart attack in January 1959, the *New York Times* observed that his "personal stamp of bigness and flamboyance" typified American film for four decades and credited his success to a combination of "flair for the showmanship of a Barnum with the cinematic inventiveness of a Griffith." Flamboyance and hokum are closely related, and some film historians, noting the stylistic distinction of many early DeMille films, believe that his later style may have been a deliberate artistic mutation caused by the natural selection of public taste. After all, popularizing by dumbing down and spiffing up Bible stories and historical facts is still good business, and DeMille was, from his earliest days, a shrewd businessman with one eye always on the box office.

DeMille's affectations—his style if you will—defined filmmaking in his time. He lived grandly in a mansion in Hollywood's then-popular Laughlin Park. He was a loving and generous father and husband but stereotypically stubborn and ruthless in business, and his word was final. A chair boy, whose only job in the late 1940s was to be certain DeMille's chair was under his ample derriere whenever the director chose to sit, recalls that he missed once, and the director landed in the dust. "You'll never work in this town again," DeMille shouted . . . and he didn't. DeMille's costume of puttees and high riding boots (to support ankles fatigued by standing on a set twelve hours a day and initially as protection against the rattlers that roamed about his first home in Hollywood), the hand-cranked camera, and his huge megaphones (for controlling huge crowds of extras in those days before electronic amplification) became icons of moviemaking for a generation. As Charlton Heston, forever DeMille's Moses, once said, in his time he was "Mr. Movies."

Cecil Blount DeMille, raised in Brooklyn, New York, and New Jersey, was born during a family vacation in Ashfield, Massachusetts, on August 12, 1881. His father, Henry, was a sometime actor and playwright, writing the first of a series of plays for the famed Broadway producer David Belasco when Cecil was born. Henry was also a lay Episcopal preacher, and every day he read to Cecil and his older brother, William, from the Bible as well as romantic novels. Although Henry De Mille* died when Cecil was only twelve, by then he had given his son a grounding in many of the elements that would define his later films: a romantically overblown love of the classics and a devotion to the Bible (especially as illustrated by Gustave Doré in a treasured book, many of whose images were later copied in DeMille's religious films).

After Henry's death, Cecil's mother, Beatrice, turned their home into a girls' school to pay the bills and sent Cecil to the Pennsylvania Military College. In 1889, Cecil enrolled in the American Academy of Dramatic Arts in New York City and, after graduation, embarked on a stage career with Belasco. He also met and married a fellow actor, Constance Adams, who would be his domestic compass and devoted companion throughout the ups and downs of his life and career (including a fair number of extramarital affairs).

In relating his memories of his marriage, DeMille, certainly unconscious of the implications, once admitted that he first became enchanted with Constance when he saw her feet as she was walking up

---

*Cecil spelled his surname DeMille or, in the case of his Paramount Studio address, deMille; his father, brother, and the rest of the family spelled it De Mille.

a staircase. Later, in his great days in Hollywood, DeMille's apparent foot fetish, mild but nevertheless motivating, was an open secret. Actresses learned to literally lead with their feet if they wanted a job. The most famous incident involved twenty-nine-year-old Paulette Goddard, who, when the director was casting *North West Mounted Police* (1940), walked into his office at Paramount studios completely made up for the part of the sexy female lead and slapped a bare foot on his desk. She got the job. And although the idea has been attributed to a number of people, including Douglas Fairbanks, Mary Pickford, and theater owner Sid Graumann, it was probably DeMille's suggestion that Graumann immortalize Hollywood's famous by asking them to imprint their feet in the soft cement in front of his newly opened Chinese Theater (now Mann's Chinese Theater), starting a tradition that created one of the most popular tourist attractions in Hollywood.

DeMille, who arrived in Hollywood in 1913, was a relative latecomer, and as with many early moviemakers, economics had motivated his move. The New York stage had fallen on hard times, and he and his friend Jesse L. Lasky (a former vaudevillian and producer of musicals) were nearly broke when they met with Lasky's brother-in-law Samuel Goldfish (later renamed Samuel Goldwyn), a glove salesman. DeMille had decided to move to Mexico, where he thought he might fight in the revolution, but Goldfish suggested a less dangerous career that also interested him—the movies—and DeMille seized on the idea. Within a few days the trio had formed a company (the Jesse L. Lasky Feature Play Company), corralled a star (Dustin Farnum), and bought their first property, a play written for Broadway by Edwin Milton Royal a decade and a half earlier named *The Squaw Man*. Lasky was president, Goldfish was business manager, and DeMille was director general, despite the fact he had never been inside one of the era's improvised motion picture studios.

As reflected in the company's title, they decided that all their films would be feature length (four or five twelve-to-twenty-minute reels) rather than the one- or two-reelers then common. They also decided to make their movie, not in New Jersey where most Westerns were then filmed, but in Flagstaff, Arizona, both for the authentic western setting and in hopes of escaping the notice of Edison's Motion Picture Patents

Company (the Trust). On arrival, DeMille immediately rejected Flagstaff (it was too "built up," a range war was in progress, it was raining, and DeMille said that it didn't look like Wyoming where the movie was set. With his cameraman and Farnum, he went on to Los Angeles where the group was besieged by location offers. They chose one that offered a "fine laboratory" in what DeMille described as a "somnolent" development called Hollywood, then proclaiming itself "The Gem of the Foothills."

Although the laboratory turned out to be only a barn at what is now the northeast corner of Selma and Vine, DeMille signed a lease (with the proviso that the horses and carriage already housed there could remain), finished casting his film, found locations he liked. Despite a story that he filmed it in Green River, Wyoming, apparently DeMille made his movie (for fifteen thousand dollars) entirely in Hollywood and the countryside surrounding Los Angeles. Although forced to wear galoshes or putting his feet in a wastebasket to keep them dry whenever the horses were watered in the studio/barn DeMille was learning how to produce, direct, and then edit a movie. The barn, after two moves, is today preserved as a California State landmark and museum near the Hollywood Bowl; the rest of the studio complex DeMille quickly added was demolished long ago. Soon Constance and their first child, Cecilia, joined the director in a large thirty-dollar-a-month house in the Cahuenga Pass (where the Hollywood Freeway would one day be built). Success came fast. The very essence of early filmmaking was speed—speed in getting to the point of a plot and speed in completing the film. Some studios were actually capable of turning out four or five two-reelers (films that ran for twenty to thirty minutes) a day. DeMille's output of longer films never rose above one a month in those hectic days and soon settled in at an average of four or five a year, but what he was turning out was enormously successful. The Squaw Man made $225,000, fifteen times its cost. Within a year he had made eight movies, among them The Virginian, The Call of the North, and The Girl of the Golden West, and had become a well-known name in the tiny film colony.

The following year he made one of the most popular of his early films, The Cheat (with its notorious scene where the young Sessue Hayakawa brands the heroine on her shoulder), and was making thousands of dollars a week at a time when the average U.S. family income was less than a thousand dollars a year.

He did what most successful directors and film stars did then and have done ever since: he bought a fancy car (a dove gray Locomobile, then one of the best), a fancy house (a large colonial in Laughlin Park), and a weekend hideaway—a six-hundred-acre ranch in the far reaches of the San Fernando Valley where he relaxed on weekends feeding deer and taking long walks through the sage-covered rocky hills; he named it Paradise. Soon Paradise got what was becoming the sine qua non of Hollywood residential one-upmanship—a swimming pool. This one was made by damming the creek that ran through the ranch. The ranch was also furnished with several huge log cabins for his family and guests, including a clubhouse with an 1,800-square-foot living room filled with Navajo rugs and trophies, all protected after 1927 by a pair of iron gates from the set of his film *The King of Kings*. No telephone, though, at least in the beginning. And like many other Hollywood successes, he eventually bought a yacht, a 106-foot diesel schooner named the *Seaward*.

Like so many film parvenus, DeMille also bought culture, but not just any culture; his had huge box-office potential. In her time the Metropolitan opera star Geraldine Farrar, like tenor Enrico Caruso, was loved by the public. She was also obsessively adored by her fans, especially thousands of young women (nicknamed "Gerry flappers") who greeted her every appearance with near hysteria. DeMille cast Farrar in four films, the most popular being the silent (but histrionically vivid) version of her most popular operatic role, *Carmen* (1915). How DeMille induced her to do it stands as an early example of the way the film industry dealt and still deals with celebrity: basically by giving them anything they want.

For Farrar, this meant a private railroad car (complete with a piano) for her, her retinue, and her current boyfriend, for each trip to and from California; a red carpet at the station with a welcoming committee that included the mayor of Los Angeles and a chorus of young girls throwing rose petals; an elegant Hispano-Suiza motorcar at her disposal; a lavish house plus an entire bungalow on the set for her use; and as the clincher, a fee of two dollars per minute of daylight for every day she was in Hollywood plus a share of the profits.

It was worth it. *Carmen* was a gigantic success, and unlike later opera stars who tried films, Farrar was wonderful in a film that stands up well even today. Her next film, *Joan the Woman,* was somewhat less successful. Nevertheless, it was a precursor of the grand DeMille epics to come, with the heroic saint viewed more or less as the girl next door (one critic called it "Joan at home with pots and pans") surrounded by a cast of thousands filling some of the most impressive sets built up to that time. As an interesting footnote, DeMille directed *Joan* via the industry's first use of telephones, becoming the first director to use electronic means to relay his commands instead of the then-ubiquitous megaphone.

Soon DeMille was on to making *Romance of the Redwoods,* his first and somewhat contentious collaboration with the already famous Mary Pickford (he paid her eighty thousand dollars), and *Male and Female* with Gloria Swanson. The director would make six films with Swanson, maintaining a friendship that lasted until his death forty years later. That was ten years after they appeared together in *Sunset Boulevard* (1950), writer-director Billy Wilder's baroquely macabre tribute to filmdom's past, in which the actress uttered the line that would turn their individual legends into Hollywood myth: "Alright, Mr. DeMille; I'm ready for my close-up."

Although Swanson also starred in the first of DeMille's religious films, the maudlin *Something to Think About* (1920), his most important early biblical epic came three years later with his first version of *The Ten Commandments.* To make it DeMille's way required the services of twenty-five hundred actors and extras, including troops from the Eleventh Cavalry standing in for the Egyptian army, and hundreds of Orthodox Jews cast in the Exodus sequence as, well, Orthodox Jews (he believed only a real Jew could convey the angst of the Exodus). DeMille also hired nearly five thousand animals and recruited a company of army cooks (after the Orthodox Jewish extras understandably refused a ham dinner dished out by DeMille's commissary, he brought in a kosher kitchen for the remainder of the sequence). Everyone lived at a self-contained "Camp DeMille" in the central California desert.

In the best D. W. Griffith tradition ("He was the teacher of us all," DeMille said often), the director intercut his historic story with a moralistic modern melodrama, which of course demanded additional sets and locations. Naturally the film became a logistical and financial nightmare. Since it also marked DeMille's pioneering use of Technicolor (in the movie's opening biblical sequences), the budget easily soared over one million dollars. But when the picture finally opened at Graumann's Egyptian theater in Hollywood December 4, 1923 (and at the George M. Cohan Theater in New York two and a half weeks later), the public loved it.

His biggest challenge, and the one DeMille felt was the most important of his life, was yet to come. *The King of Kings* (1927) was the most expensive film ever made at that time and would remain so for years thereafter. The problems confronted in making it were monumental. Many of them were problems with the cast (an alcoholic H. B. Warner as Jesus, Dorothy Cummings in the middle of a scandalous and highly publicized divorce as the Virgin Mary), the animals (a hundred doves had to be trained to fly in formation), and extras (every mounted legionnaire was a real cowboy). As usual at this point in De-Mille's career, the logistics were also daunting. Filming was spread over many inconvenient locations (a passenger steamer was needed to take the cast, crew, and props to Catalina for the filming of the scenes by the Sea of Galilee). Costs soared to an unheard of $2.5 million, and bankers scrambled for additional funds, eventually forcing DeMille into a short-lived shotgun partnership with Pathé films and others to pay the bills.

Altogether more than three hundred *miles* of film were shot. These included the lashing and crucifixion of Christ, which formed the highly unorthodox centerpiece for a Christmas Eve press open house on the Hollywood set, after which everyone—cast, crew, and press—stood with bowed heads for five minutes of meditation accompanied by organ music. The crucifixion scene, based on a Gustav Doré etching from DeMille's childhood book, was directed in part by D. W. Griffith during an impromptu visit to the set.

After an immensely successful premiere in New York, *The King of Kings* opened as the first booking at Sid Graumann's new Chinese Theater in Hollywood. The hoopla of this opening would set a style for generations. As a hundred thousand onlookers jammed Hollywood

Boulevard outside the theater, screaming themselves hoarse, stars arrived for the twenty-two-dollar-per-ticket event. D. W. Griffith was the master of ceremonies, and Mary Pickford pushed the button that opened the theater's curtain. Unfortunately, Graumann chose to precede the movie with a live and endlessly long biblical prologue, and most of the exhausted audience left at the intermission of the two-and-a-half-hour epic. DeMille was inconsolable. Will Hays, Hollywood's new censor, didn't help much when he suggested to the director, "The only thing left is for you to get run over on the way home." Fortunately he survived the two-mile trip to Laughlin Park. *The King of Kings* survived as well, eventually becoming one of the most successful films of the director's career.

By 1928, DeMille had gotten out of his forced partnership and settled into offices at MGM, which he decorated with props from several films, including the Grail used for the Last Supper in *The King of Kings* and spears from *The Ten Commandments*. There he would challenge the swiftly emerging sound era with *Dynamite* (memorable for a dance scene in a zeppelin that has broken away from its mooring during a storm) and a talkie remake of *The Squaw Man* before moving back to Paramount. More historical epics would come, including *The Sign of the Cross* (1932), *Cleopatra* two years later (both starring Claudette Colbert, who was surprisingly unmemorable as the Queen of Egypt in a bath of ass's milk), and *The Crusades* starring Loretta Young.

DeMille had interests other than film as well. He had discovered a passion for flying in an ill-fated attempt to get a commission to fight in World War I, and in 1920, in partnership with a few like-minded friends, cofounded California's first commercial airline, which flew out of an airport named for the director at what is today the busy corner of Wilshire Boulevard and Fairfax. He also introduced air advertising (by dropping leaflets from his planes), aerial mapping, and an early airborne watch for the wildfires that still plague Southern California. DeMille also became a household name through radio, hosting for nine years (from 1936 until a union dispute forced his departure in 1944) the hour-long Lux Radio Theater on CBS to which an audience of more than thirty million tuned in weekly to hear famous stars performing condensed versions of film classics.

DeMille's production slowed appreciably as he entered his sixties in 1941 and began encountering problems with his health. He completed only four films during that entire decade: *Reap the Wild Wind, The Story of Dr. Wassell, Unconquered,* and *Samson and Delilah.* In the 1950s, he completed only two films: *The Greatest Show on Earth* (bringing DeMille his only "craft" Oscar; he also won two honorary Oscars) and his final picture, the new version of *The Ten Commandments.*

The 1940s also brought DeMille the one unmitigated tragedy in his life. On March 15, 1941, during a visit by his daughter Katherine and son-in-law Anthony Quinn, the couple's three-year-old son, Christopher, toddled away from his nanny and drowned in the pool at W. C. Field's adjoining home. Although the Quinn's were to have other children before divorcing in 1965, they never got over their first son's death, and even now Anthony refuses to speak of it. Both were too grief-stricken to attend Christopher's funeral; it was left to the child's grandfather to lay him to rest.

The relationship between DeMille and his son-in-law was highly charged from the very beginning; neither could do anything right as far as the other was concerned. Whenever DeMille invited Quinn to dine with him at Paramount, the actor saw it as a Machiavellian effort to engender jealousy and ultimately rejection from his fellow actors. When DeMille recut a remake of Quinn's 1938 film *The Buccaneer,* a first-time directing effort by the actor, Quinn saw it as a personal rebuke. In any event, the remake, DeMille's last screen credit (a production credit), was a disaster.

Not long before DeMille's death, Quinn tried to make peace with him, but "when we finally could see past our conceits and our fears, it was too late," Quinn has written.

On the night of January 20, 1959, DeMille's daughter Cecilia and her husband dropped by for a visit. After they left, DeMille scribbled the opening words of the Episcopal funeral service on a piece of paper and added, "After those words are spoken, what am I? I am only what I have accomplished. How much good have I spread? How much evil have I spread? For whatever I am a moment after death—a spirit, a soul, a bodiless mind—I shall have to look back and forward, for I have to take with me both." He died later that night.

When pallbearers, including Samuel Goldwyn and Adolph Zukor, carried DeMille's casket into Hollywood's tiny Saint Stephen's Episcopal Church for the funeral two days later, they passed, framed on the wall, the red granite tablets Charlton Heston as Moses brought down the mountain in the director's final film. Following DeMille's meticulous habit, they had been hewn from the heights of Mount Sinai itself and inscribed with the Ten Commandments written in early Bronze Age Canaanite lettering from the prophet's own era.

A cynic might suggest that DeMille's last words sound too much like something from one of his films. Perhaps they do. But they also sound exactly like the way a person who had succeeded beyond all measure in creating Hollywood's worldwide cultural influence might reflect at this extremity of his life. In any event, for good or evil, his legacy has influenced the way films have been made ever since. From tacky historical epics like *Cleopatra* (1962) starring Elizabeth Taylor to sci-fi Westerns like *Star Wars* to action-adventure sagas beyond naming, they all owe something to Cecil B. DeMille's grandiose visions. He, far more than D. W. Griffith, "showed the way."

The home of costume designer Adrian and actress Janet Gaynor (winner of the first Best Actress Oscar in 1927 for *Seventh Heaven*) in Whitley Heights was once described by Greta Garbo's lover Mercedes de Acosta as "more a stage set than a residence . . . as unreal as cardboard." For years one of Hollywood's most famous residences, it was also home to authors William Faulkner (who rented an attached studio) and Ben Hecht, as well as conductor Leonard Bern-

You Were Where You Lived—
Mr. Whitley's Neighborhood

Back in the era of silent films, among the two best addresses in Los Angeles were Hancock Park and Whitley Heights.

Hancock Park, which still exists, was never particularly popular with the film crowd, nor was the film crowd particularly popular with Hancock Park's residents, who until a generation ago were basically members of the city's WASP establishment. They had their own upscale stores (the Broadway Wilshire, where future star Angela Lansbury once worked as a saleslady), their own very upscale restaurant (Perino's, where little spice and no garlic were ever allowed), their own churches (among them two-thousand-seat, neo-Gothic Immanuel Presbyterian, where ushers in tailcoats seated the all-white congregation), and, of course, a wall surrounding the community—one of the first in America—to keep out the hoi polloi.

Whitley Heights was a different matter altogether. It

was founded by a Canadian real estate developer, banker, and entrepreneur named Hobart Johnstone Whitley, who should be more famous than he is. Arriving in Los Angeles in 1893 from the Oklahoma Territory where he had created several frontier towns (including Oklahoma City), Whitley not only built the railroad that linked downtown Los Angeles to the San Fernando Valley but with typical entrepreneurial flair then founded the cities that railroad would serve, including Van Nuys, Studio City (then called Lankershim), Sherman Oaks, and Canoga Park. He also assisted Harvey Wilcox in laying out his suburb of Hollywood and was responsible for changing the name of Prospect Avenue to Hollywood Boulevard.

The neighborhood that would become Whitley Heights was first recorded when Whitley bought a steep eucalyptus-and pine-covered hill on the flanks of the Santa Monica Mountains in 1901. Two years later he built a mission-style pavilion atop its western crest so that prospective investors could enjoy the spectacular views from his planned community. Then nothing much happened until the end of World War I, when the developer sent an architect to Italy to study classic buildings. Whitley subsequently passed his vision on to an entire battery of architects, who in the course of designing some two hundred houses introduced a Mediterranean look that eventually became synonymous with the Southern California lifestyle (Whitley's buyers were given a discount if they built quickly and in the chosen style). The "look," still popular, included arched doorways, huge picture windows, overscaled terra-cotta or concrete mantels, ornate wrought-iron gates, balconies, balustrades, sconces, and stippled interior walls. Many of the houses also had courtyards, which would inspire Cecil B. DeMille's architect and designer friend, Frederick Zwebell, and his wife, Nina, to create a series of legendary courtyard buildings in Hollywood, which themselves spawned countless imitations. For himself Whitley erected a mansion in an elegant Palladian style not at all like the Mediterranean look of the rest of the neighborhood.

Whitley Heights quickly grew to resemble an Italian hill town, its villas, roofed with red-clay tiles, stacked one atop the other on the narrow, curved streets under which were buried, far in advance of other developments of the time, the power and telephone lines. The four levels of the hill were linked by six staircases, some still in use, and heavy posts were connected by chains to keep cars from rolling down the hills. Not surprisingly, the development was immediately popular with the film community, most of whom worked within a couple of miles.

It often comes as a shock to fans of Hollywood's history to discover how small an area contained the birth and early growth of what would become one of the world's greatest industries. It's no more than a mile or so from Cecil B. DeMille's Laughlin Place mansion, for example, to the original location of the barn where he started making films in 1913. It's less than that from Whitley Heights to what became identified in romantic legend (if not fact) as the center of town: the corner of Hollywood and Vine. Nearly everything was contained within a circumference of a couple of miles: studios, residences, restaurants, hotels, churches, stores, banks, and—after liquor was allowed in the formerly dry community—saloons and clubs. You could, if you wanted, walk to anything you needed.

In fact, walking was often the easiest way to get around. Franklin Avenue in the teens was a picturesque dirt road sheltered by then-ubiquitous pepper trees. Those trees were among the first victims of Hollywood's growth; they were chopped down after automobiles arrived in significant numbers, and it was discovered that their fallen fruit discolored the finish of the cars parked below.

By the 1920s, tour buses were chugging up the steep hills of Whitley Heights to show tourists the homes of silent film greats like Francis X. Bushman, Harold Lloyd, Charlie Chaplin, Wallace Reid, Richard Barthelmess, and, most famously, Rudolph Valentino, who could often be spotted, clad in riding togs, walking his two mastiffs and his Doberman along the narrow roads. Even the local residents were impressed; it's said that wives used to hustle their husbands off to work early and rush out to water their gardens in time to say hello to the Latin Lover as he passed by.

Although the rise of Beverly Hills after the advent of sound drew many actors and celebrities westward, many silent stars and a few other independent-minded celebrities chose to continue living in the now quaint neighborhood. Over the years they included Bette Davis, Jean Harlow, Greta Garbo, Marie Dressler, Maurice Chevalier, Rosalind Russell, Carmen Miranda, Leo G. Carroll, William Powell and Carole Lombard (during their brief marriage in the 1930s), and Tyrone Power and Hermione Gingold, both of whom lived in Francis X. Bushman's famed mansion, Topside, which burned down in the 1960s. Dressler, one of the silent film era's greatest character actors, remembered the appeal of Whitley Heights in her autobiography: "From my second story veranda, I could see acre upon acre of green California grass and bright-hued California flowers. I could watch whole regiments of royal palms march down white avenues. I lived on my little porch." She loved it so much that she bought a second house and added a swimming pool, once said to be the first of the tens of thousands in Los Angeles.

Gloria Swanson lived in the Villa Vallombrosa in Whitley Heights while making *Sunset Boulevard*. Earlier the residence of Janet Gaynor, the costume designer Adrian, and William Faulkner (who worked in Hollywood in the 1930s), it was later home to writer Ben Hecht and conductor Leonard Bernstein. Mercedes de Acosta, Greta Garbo's lover, once recalled a dinner at the house, which she described as looking "more like a stage set that a residence . . . as unreal as cardboard," during Adrian's residence. During cocktails, a large boulder rolled down the mountain, broke through the living room wall, and came to rest among the guests. "This was the kind of thing that could only happen in Hollywood," wrote de Acosta.

About a third of Whitley Heights was lost in the mid-1950s when wrecking balls and bulldozers cleared the way for the Hollywood Freeway, but there is enough left to get a feeling for what it once was—163 houses and three small apartment buildings, to be exact, all now preserved as one of the few communities in America on the National Register of Historic Places. But what's been lost to progress is a tragedy for film buffs. The home Valentino lived in longest is gone, and so is Bette Davis's, cleared for a Hollywood museum that never happened. One in a series of homes that Charlie Chaplin rented in the area on his rise to fame was also destroyed.

But enough is there to provide a time travel trip back to Hollywood's silent era.

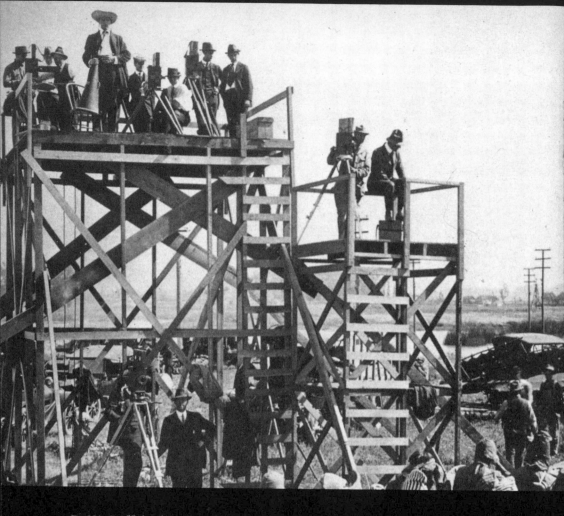

D. W. Griffith, director of *Intolerance* (1916), the most famous and influential American movie of the era, stands high atop the camera platform built for filming the movie's celebrated Babylonian sequence. The neighborhood, near the intersection of Sunset and Hollywood Boulevards, wouldn't long remain as empty as it appears in the background.

Intolerance and the Fickleness of Fame

Hollywood abounds in ironies, none more poignant perhaps than those in the last years of the man once the film capital's most famous director, David Wark Griffith. By 1948, he was largely forgotten by the industry he had essentially fathered. But whenever he looked from the window of his room at the Hotel Knickerbocker, his last home, he could easily see where he began the rise to his once nearly unimaginable fame, clearly visible less than two miles—but an unbridgeable two decades—away.

There on the horizon, at the intersection of Sunset and Hollywood Boulevards, was once the studio where he made *The Birth of a Nation* (1914), the movie in which President Woodrow Wilson said Griffith "wrote history with lightning." It was also—and remains—one of the most controversial films ever made. A look at the Civil War and the horrors of the Reconstruction years from a Southern point of view, it was directly responsible for the vigorous rebirth of the Ku Klux Klan at the time. Across the street once stood the two-hundred-foot-high towers of Griffiths's Babylon, the set for the most famous sequence in his 1916 epic *Intolerance,* then the most gigantic ever built in America. It was the movie that would, rightly or wrongly, also mythologize him as the creator of modern filmmaking.

Until 1920, when the city of Los Angeles ordered them torn down, those towers would loom high above the neighborhood's small, shingle-covered bungalows, decaying in the Southern California sun. And for the last twenty years of his life, with the possible exception of his *Abraham Lincoln* (1931), Griffith's fame would decay as sadly and relentlessly. Unlike the pioneering storytelling and filmmaking techniques he created or refined, Griffith failed to move with the times. He became an anachronism, an old-fashioned embarrassment in his own community.

Griffith died on July 24, 1948, after suffering a cerebral hemorrhage in that lonely room where, to keep them cool, he often stored apples and sodas on the sill of the window from which he could see his past. (Not far from Griffith's room Elvis Presley later lived and was inspired to write "Heartbreak Hotel.")

The only celebrity who visited the funeral home was a director whose fame also stemmed from creating popular epics: Cecil B. De-Mille. A few more of Hollywood's famous, some of whom, like Lionel Barrymore and Mack Sennett, owed their film-career starts to him, showed up for the funeral in the half-filled Masonic Temple. Some, like Mary Pickford, whose career was launched by Griffith when she was sixteen, didn't show up at all. Many of the funeral guests shunned honorary pallbearers like Louis B. Mayer (who, after his career change from junk dealer to film exhibitor, made a fortune from *The Birth of a Nation)* and Samuel Goldwyn, both of whom could have given Griffith work in his later years but didn't.

When he was laid to rest in a tiny, rural graveyard in his native Kentucky, next to his father who first entranced him with the tales of Confederate derring-do that would inspire much of *The Birth of a Nation,* only one star of the many who owed their careers to him was there: Lillian Gish.

It was a four-hanky story Griffith would have loved filming.

D. W. Griffith was born on January 22, 1875, in La Grange, Kentucky. His father, Jacob, died when David was ten, after a life spent as a sometime politician, full-time farmer, and passionate Confederate loyalist. David's mother, Mary, was the quiet, affectionate anchor of the family.

Griffith wanted to be an actor from an early age, and for a number of years trod the boards in Louisville and on the road. In 1905, he first visited Los Angeles, cast as an Indian in a stage adaptation of Helen Hunt Jackson's then-popular novel *Ramona* (Griffith would later use it for a film). The following year he married a fellow actor, Linda Arvidson, and moved to New York City where he tried his hand unsuccessfully as a playwright and looked for acting work. At the suggestion of a friend he ran into in the old Forty-second Street Automat, Griffith decided to look into films—not as an actor but as a scenario writer—to tide himself and Linda over the winter. (Before scripts, demanded by sound, writers wrote scenarios.) It was as an actor that he was hired, first by Edwin Porter (who four years earlier had made *The Great Train Robbery*) to play the lead in a forgettable film, and then, at age thirty-three, by the Biograph Company as both scenarist and actor. The job changed his life.

Biograph was by 1907 already the best of the early filmmakers, but like most, it was a small, informal community of largely anonymous talent grinding out two one-reelers a week from its studio in an East Fourteenth Street brownstone. Among those talents was cameraman Billy Bitzer, who, when Griffith's stage-trained acting proved too overdone for the intimacy of film, suggested that Griffith step in for a sick director. It was also Bitzer who explained to the rookie director how to make his first film, laying out the scenario on a piece of laundry shirt–cardboard. Never, even in the glory days to come when Bitzer and Griffith would essentially write filmmaking's first grammar, would Griffith work from a written scenario.

And what days they were as commercial success made taking chances possible. Most of Griffith's hundreds of films for Biograph (141 in 1909 alone!) made a lot of money, largely because he somehow knew what the relatively unsophisticated audience of the time wanted and how to deliver it.

One thing Griffith believed was that audiences wanted longer films, films that told a more complete story. So in 1913, spurred by the example of the large-scale films being turned out in Italy, and permanently settled into making movies in the Southern California sun, he made *Judith of Bethulia* near the present Los Angeles suburb of Chatsworth in the San Fernando Valley. It was a four-reel biblical epic and one of the first to star the talent who would become Griffith's most famous discovery, Lillian Gish. It also went overbudget by 100 percent, causing such a row between Griffith and the Biograph management that he formed his own company—and took many of Biograph's leading talents along with him. Announcing his new company in a now famous advertisement, he took credit for introducing the fade-out (apparently true, although some film historians differ), the close-up, the long shot, crosscutting, and something called "restraint in expression," certainly related to his earlier troubles toning down his stage gestures for film.

An amazing series of pictures followed that would make D. W. Griffith the most famous director in the world: *The Birth of a Nation, Intolerance, Hearts of the World, Broken Blossoms, Way Down East,* and *Orphans of the Storm.* The most famous, because it was the most infamous as well, was *The Birth of a Nation.*

Based on a racist jeremiad of a book and play by Thomas Dixon called *The Clansman,* the saga of a Southern family torn by the Civil War, appealed to Griffith as a chance to write history from the loser's point of view. It was unquestionably also an emotional response based on memories of the heroic reminiscences of his father, a twice-wounded Confederate colonel. The movie was made in locations in and around Los Angeles, including Griffith Park, the pine forest near Big Bear Lake, and the countryside near Whittier where the movie's climactic ride of the Klansmen was filmed. One of the extras in that scene was John Ford, whose future career as a director nearly ended that day when, blinded by his Klan bedsheet, he was knocked from his horse by an overhanging branch; Griffith himself revived him with a shot of brandy.

The Clansman, as it was called in its early release, cost a then-astronomical one hundred thousand dollars to make and promote. Driven by notoriety (including a failed effort by the NAACP to suppress the film entirely), it would make a fortune. How much? No one will ever know exactly because of the standard financial shenanigans employed by exhibitors of the era. The best estimates are somewhere in the neighborhood of sixty million dollars. Adjusted for inflation, that would be around nine hundred million of today's dollars, making *The Birth of a Nation* one of the all-time most successful movies ever made.

Griffith's next film was in many ways both his greatest and his clumsiest. Before the premiere of *The Birth of a Nation,* Griffith had made a small movie based on a Dickension story of a young couple whose lives are destroyed by a strike. Called *The Mother and the Law,* it was never released, and the name was assigned to two new stories of injustice Griffith planned to film. Coincidently, he saw *Cabiria,* one of the hugely successful historical epics then being made in Italy. He was impressed by the ambitious scope of the film, which combined the intimacy of close-up shots with the panoramic grandeur of the burning of the Roman fleet and Hannibal's crossing of the Alps with seemingly thousands of extras and live elephants. Somehow the idea occurred to Griffith of filming a sort of cinematic sermon condemning intolerance by intercutting four stories: the heroic resistance of the Babylonians to the Persian invaders, the Saint Bartholomew's Day massacre of the French Huguenots, the original story of the young couple torn asunder by social violence, and three tableaux from the life of Christ. Working as always without a script, Griffith quite literally had no idea when to stop or start on this gargantuan project. He just kept filming, shooting more than a hundred miles of film, which eventually was edited down to three hours and fifteen minutes. Then and for years afterward, *Intolerance* was the longest film ever made.

Griffith's colleagues couldn't figure it out, and neither could audiences, after the effect of the stupendous visuals wore off. But, the film will live as a benchmark in film history, not for the stories it tried to tell, but for the way Griffith told them. Audiences were especially stunned by the sets for the fall of Babylon, with its thirty-foot-high elephants (a direct steal from *Cabiria*) and its images based on familiar biblical paintings. Few who ever saw *Intolerance* can forget the scene where the crowded steps of Babylon are first glimpsed from a great distance, then come closer and closer as the camera descends in a gigantically long tracking shot, down and down and down, ending atop Belshazzar's bacchanal. That sort of shot is done all the time these days with a camera crane, but when Griffith did it in 1914, they didn't exist. How did he do it?

Griffith and cameraman Bitzer first tried a balloon for the camera and cameraman, but it proved too unstable. Then engineer Allen Dwan, later a director himself, suggested mounting the camera on an open elevator that was itself mounted on a narrow-gauge flatcar on tracks leading to the three-hundred-foot-deep set. So as the elevator was slowly lowered, workmen pushed the flatcar forward. It was the movies' first crane shot and even today one of the most memorable.

By now World War I was on in all its fury, and because Griffith was easily the most famous film director alive, the British invited him to visit and film footage for use in propaganda pictures. He was the only American filmmaker to visit the front. For Griffith, however, storytelling on celluloid was by then becoming more real than the real thing; he would subsequently film frontline action on the Salisbury Plain in England and back home in Hollywood.

Some of that war footage found its way into his next feature, *Hearts of the World*, a melodramatic look at four war-torn years in a French family's life. The story, a pastiche of lost and found love, is mostly memorable for Lillian Gish's wonderful mad scene as she wanders through a battlefield searching for her lover, and the terrific patriotic ending as rank after rank of American soldiers march across the screen. (One side note: In *Hearts of the World,* Gish's child was played by Ben Alexander, who would become familiar to a later generation as Sgt. Joe Friday's sidekick on Dragnet.)

Griffith's next film, *Broken Blosssoms,* was something altogether different; for all intents and purposes it was the first film noir. The intimacy of its story about an abused girl (Lillian Gish) and the Chinaman who tries to rescue her with tragic consequences (Richard Barthelmess) was thrown into high relief by the epic splendor of the films that came before and after.

In early 1919, Griffith joined Mary Pickford, her fiancé Douglas Fairbanks, and Charlie Chaplin in forming United Artists to control the distribution of their films. For Fairbanks, Pickford, and Chaplin it was a great success, not for Griffith, who had nothing to distribute that wasn't previously contracted. He also decided to open the only studio he ever owned—a mistake in hindsight—in New York's Westchester County, far away from Hollywood, which since the war had left Europe's industries in ruins was now the world's cinema capital.

For a while it still appeared that Griffith could do no wrong, especially when the first film made in his new studio was released in 1920. It was far grander than *Broken Blossoms* and hugely profitable. *Way Down East* is a creaky story of a wronged woman (Lillian Gish again) who overcomes social prejudice and near death to find true love (Richard Barthelmess again). The film's final sequence, a tremendously long chase through a blizzard and across an ice-jammed river as Barthelmess races to rescue Gish, unconscious on an ice floe, was challenging to make (Gish claimed she was on the ice twenty times a day for three weeks and that once her hair froze solid). It was, and still is, breathtaking to watch, and in the opinion of many film scholars it still stands as one of cinema's greatest climaxes.

For all the technical innovations, for all the spectacle and the exciting climaxes, probably the one thing that separated D. W. Griffith from everyone else—and still does—was his uncanny ability to create emotional intimacy, the genius to deliver stunning, flashing moments that bind each individual in an audience to the story on the screen. That happens in the last of his great films. It wasn't the last film he made, for Griffith's career was to continue for a number of years before finally petering out in the 1930s, but it was one of the best. *Orphans of the Storm* was less what it appeared to be (a convoluted history of the French Revolution) than a human drama, the story of a pair of sisters, one blind (Lillian Gish and her sister Dorothy, who played the blind sibling), separated by circumstances and the turmoil of the time.

Despite the formulistic drama (including a Griffith signature rescue chase, an improbably happy ending, and, of course, the restoration of Dorothy Gish's sight), there is one scene when Griffith, the one-time stage actor—and, of course, Lillian Gish—incontestably proved to the world that great acting can happen in movies too. It happens when Gish's character thinks she hears the voice of her long-lost sister begging in the street below her room. Griffith films it with one of his trademark backlit, intimate close-ups, the camera frozen as Gish first dismisses the idea and then, as her sister's voice continues, realizes that a miracle has indeed happened. The intensity is so palpable one hardly breathes.

Griffith would make a few more films, most notably a biography of Abraham Lincoln. But *Way Down East* was his last box-office success. The times had moved past him. Sound, which he never really understood, arrived along with a new generation of filmmakers who took his many technical advances and streamlined them. But none were ever to improve on the many moments when his emotional lightning struck the hearts of filmgoers.

Rudolph Valentino sets out from the long-gone Villa Valentino to walk one of his mastiffs on the steep streets of Whitley Heights during a summer morning in 1923. The car is his French Voisin, with his trademark cobra hood ornament, and bought in Paris.

Rudolph Valentino, His Villa, and the Wife from Hell

In December 1921, more than a year before *The Four Horsemen of the Apocalypse* and *The Sheik* were released, catapulting him to a fame probably unmatched by any leading man, Rudolph Valentino scraped together the down payment for his first real home in Hollywood. It was an eight-room, Spanish-style house on a steeply sloping acre of land in the Whitley Heights development. It was also in serious disrepair.

Since he and his second wife, actress Natacha Rambova, couldn't afford new furniture, they carted Rambova's belongings from her Sunset Boulevard duplex up to the house, had the gas and water turned on, and two days before Christmas, moved in. All they had to furnish the large living room was a single chair, so they filled the empty space with a Christmas tree and home-made wreaths.

They didn't take Zela to the new house; she was the pet baby lion that on at least one occasion had chased away a burglar from Rambova's apartment. Zela had grown to the point where she had to be sent to an exotic animal farm. Both missed her, but her absence gave Valentino an idea for the perfect Christmas present for Natacha: a Pekingese puppy, stuffed in a stocking hanging from the mantel on the room's huge fireplace.

By their later standards it was a bleak holiday season, but both would remember it as the happiest time they shared in a marriage that ended within four years, overwhelmed by Valentino's fame and his decision to manage his own career instead of delegating the responsibility to Rambova, who had played the villain too often in earlier negotiations.

Today that house is gone, a victim of the wrecker's ball making way for the Hollywood Freeway. In fact, the very existence of Valentino's Whitley Heights villa has largely vanished from Hollywood lore and is generally unknown to film fans who still make pilgrimages to his more famous residence, Falcon Lair, which Valentino built in Beverly Hills in 1924 in an attempt to save his marriage. But by then Rambova had left him, and the actor moved into it alone. He lived there only a few months before his sudden death in New York on August 23, 1926, from peritonitis caused by a perforated ulcer stunned the world.

The earlier house, Villa Valentino, was his home.

Despite her exotic Russian name, Natacha Rambova was as American as apple pie. Born in January 1897 in Salt Lake City and christened Winifred Kimball Shaughnessy, she was the daughter of a former federal marshal and mining entrepreneur and his wife, a descendant of a Mormon patriarch. A privileged child, Winifred was educated in England and spent vacations in France at the famous Villa Trianon of Elsie de Wolfe in Versailles. Generally recognized as the founder of interior decorating, de Wolfe was also Winifred's aunt by marriage. Back in America, Winifred joined the Theodore Kosloff ballet studio in Los Angeles, assumed her romantically Russian-sounding name, and eventually also designed the costumes for Kosloff's grandly titled Imperial Russian Ballet when it toured America in 1916. She also began designing sets and costumes for the infant film industry.

Rambova met Valentino when he was cast as Armand in *Camille,* which was produced by and would star the famous Russian actress Alla Nazimova. Valentino and Rambova, the costume designer of the film, were instantly attracted to each other and, despite rumors that Rambova was a lesbian (her friend Nazimova was famously so) and that Valentino was gay, the couple were occasionally caught making love like cats in heat, "tigers" was the term used by one friend. Before the couple married and moved into Villa Valentino, they shared an apartment with cameraman Paul Ivano at the old Formosa Apartments (at Hollywood Boulevard and La Brea, eight blocks west of the Hotel Hollywood). Ivano recalled that one night he was awakened by a naked, still erect Valentino screaming hysterically that he had "killed Natacha." She wasn't dead, just unconscious from their vigorous lovemaking. Ivano eventually revived her by sponging her naked body, telling Valentino to stay away until she cooled down.

Theirs seemed a perfect relationship in other ways also. Valentino needed Rambova's common sense to counter his naïveté, and she loved his physical aggression, once commenting, "Rudy looks best when he's naked." She also reveled in his growing celebrity.

Valentino was born on May 6, 1895, at Castellaneta near Taranto in the boot of Italy. Like most children of noble families, albeit rural nobility, he was given a long string of names, in this case Rodolpho Alfonso Raffaelo Filiberto Guglielmi di Valentina d'Antonguolla. It was simply as Rodolpho Guglielmi that he immigrated to America in 1913, working occasionally as a waiter, a professional dancer (once supplanting Clifton Webb as the dance partner of then-celebrated Bonnie Glass), or a gardener, and often sleeping in Central Park. On the advice of a friend who—struck by the handsome youth's appearance and personality—suggested that he go into movies, Valentino hopped on a train west. (It was, in fact, the train carrying the cast and company of the Broadway show *The Passing Crowd* to Los Angeles; its star, Al Jolson, would later become the first famous voice of sound films.)

It was not as an actor but as a dancer that Valentino first got work in Hollywood, but soon he was cast in a film, *The Married Virgin*. He was paid fifty dollars, the same salary he was given for dancing in a later film, *The Rogue's Romance,* and it was based on the film footage shot of him: a dollar a foot. At a party in 1919, he met scenario writer Jean Acker, whom he soon married and divorced (Acker locked him out of her Hotel Hollywood room on their wedding night; the story is told at more length in chapter 10.

Valentino's next two films were made in New York. Before leaving Hollywood, however, he had noticed in a trade paper that Metro (before it became Metro-Goldwyn-Mayer) was going to film Vicente Blasco Ibanez's then-popular novel *The Four Horsemen of the Apocalypse*. While on the train east, Valentino read the book and thought the role of the hero, an Argentine gaucho named Julio Desnoyers who is caught up in the chaos of World War I, would be perfect for him. He contacted the studio's New York office to express his interest. Coincidently, June Mathis, the powerful scenario writer and producer of the movie, had seen the actor in *Eyes of Youth* (1919), decided he was perfect for the role, and was trying to locate him. Of such coincidences have Hollywood dreams been made for generations.

The film, which cost a then-astronomical $640,000 to make, was released in August 1922. It would eventually net four million dollars, a huge amount for the era, and make Valentino a star (its seductive tango scene, which took three days to film, was far more famous at the time than anything Fred Astaire and Ginger Rogers did later). The movie also established the reputations of Mathis and the film's director, Rex Ingram, and not so incidentally saved the financially strapped Metro Pictures.

Three months earlier Valentino and Rambova had finally gotten married in Mexicali, Mexico, accompanied by Paul Ivano and Alla Nazimova, as well as a string quartet and a military band they had picked up along the way. The event quickly turned into a festival when residents of the town discovered the great Latin star in their midst. Unfortunately, it was also a year before Valentino's divorce from Jean Acker would be finalized. A week later he pled guilty to bigamy in a Los Angeles court. Since it was Sunday and the banks were closed, he couldn't raise the ten-thousand-dollar bail and was thrown in jail like a common criminal until, later that day, bail was met by friends. After the couple and the wedding party perjured themselves testifying that the marriage had not been consummated following the wedding, the judge dropped the bigamy charge, and Rudy and Natacha were free to build a life together at Villa Valentino.

Following an extended European trip in 1923 (during which Valentino bought his often photographed Voisin motorcar, with its coiled cobra hood ornament, and Kabar, his beloved Doberman pinscher, in Paris) and buying and furnishing a lavish Park Avenue apartment in New York, the couple commenced the serious renovation and decorating of Villa Valentino. The style was up-to-date moderne except for the upstairs bedrooms, which were furnished with antiques bought in Europe (and more appropriate for the old Spanish look of the house). A sunken black marble floor was installed in the living room, to which Natacha added velvet rugs and early streamlined furniture lacquered black and red. The walls were painted yellow and hung with modern paintings.

Valentino's bathroom boasted a five-headed shower and a thronelike toilet with a carved and gilded seat. An accessory in the dressing room, which guaranteed a must-see visit by guests, was a small spray in the vanity which, when a button was pressed, squirted scent into the room. It was inspired, apparently, by a perforated floor in Seville, Spain's, Alhambra through which perfumed steam vapors rose from an underground room.

Outside, the couple added another accessory, rare at the time, which, unlike the incense machine, would become a Hollywood cliché: a six-sided swimming pool. Valentino also opted for another feature that would one day become as commonplace as the pool: a barbecue pit. It was one of the first in America and was inspired by Valentino's research for *The Sheik*. The garden also boasted a fishpond, and an aviary for Rambova's collection of finches.

Most stars of the time weren't quite so domestic; many, in fact, lived in hotels for much of their careers, eating and partying in whatever restaurants or clubs were popular at the time. Not so the Valentinos. Rambova, like many before and since, considered Hollywood a cultural wasteland, and she had no time for small talk ("Work," she once said in an oft-quoted remark, "is the one thing that makes life in Hollywood tolerable"). Keeping house was also a good way of keeping her husband on a leash, as demonstrated by her famous 1924 Christmas present to him: a platinum slave bracelet from Tiffany's. And Rambova was quite aware that many in the film capital thought of her as a black widow spider feeding on its captured mate, so she would occasionally invite journalists to Villa Valentino to see for themselves how happy the couple were.

Even if he had possessed the best public relations advisers in the business, there was little Valentino could have done to fight the slander that followed him for much of his mercurial career. Women adored him, but most men despised him. The reasons were many. They saw him as a foreign gigolo, and they laughed at his way of dress and behavior. One Chicago newspaper went so far as to call men who copied his romantic manner "pink powder puffs." This hurt him terribly. He was an accomplished actor who had a great sense of humor and could even poke fun at his reputation (in *The Eagle*); he collected rare books, had a knowledge of engineering, and loved machinery—especially cars and cameras. But he never forgot the vicious slurs. According to John dos Passos in *The Big Money* docu-novel from his *U.S.A.* trilogy, when Valentino came out of the anesthesia after the operation that revealed his peritonitis to be inoperable (and thus in those preantibiotics days fatal), he said, "Well, did I behave like a pink powder puff?"

Hearst writer Adela Rogers St. Johns tried to explain why Valentino aroused such hostility among men. "He came along as the first of the great foreign lovers," she wrote. "[A decade later] every American man was perfectly willing that his wife should be in love with [Clark] Gable, because Gable was what he would have liked to have been. But they were not willing that their wives should be in love with this foreigner, this dago."

Valentino was also one of the first Hollywood stars to buck the studio system (Famous Players–Lasky, later Paramount), and for a time this meant he was out of work. The couple paid their bills by selling tens of thousands of photographs of the star for a quarter apiece and going on a dance tour together for a beauty preparation called Mineralava. Because he was already so famous that schools would close so children could see the star when he and Rambova arrived in town, Valentino eventually won his independence. In fact, one of the most famous photos taken in Hollywood during this era was snapped in 1925 when Valentino signed a contract to make several movies for United Artists (including *The Eagle*, and what turned out to be his last film, *Son of the Sheik*).

But the contract, made without Rambova's advice, also spelled the end of the marriage. Rambova considered it an insult. So on August 13, 1925, she embarked on a "marital vacation" in New York and ultimately France. The couple would remain in contact but never saw each other again. Valentino died less than a year later; he was only thirty-one. As the train carried his body westward, people knelt on either side of the track as it passed.

Valentino was first interred in a crypt at Hollywood Memorial Cemetery belonging to June Mathis. Since Mathis died soon afterward, stricken while attending a theater performance in New York, pending settlement of Valentino's estate, his body was moved to another crypt owned by Mathis's husband. A year later he was moved to his permanent resting place, purchased by his brother, Alberto.

By the time he died, the actor who started in Hollywood at fifty dollars a picture was getting two hundred thousand plus 50 percent of the profits, but he had saved little. In his will he left Jean Acker nothing and left Natacha Rambova only one dollar. "Rudy has explained everything," Rambova said later without revealing the explanation. "I understand." Pola Negri, the sultry Polish actress who was his lover during his last year (and who after his death claimed they would have married), was not mentioned in the will at all.

For years, on the anniversary of his death, a number of women, all dressed in black, have gathered before his crypt in Hollywood Memorial Cemetery, since renamed Hollywood Forever Cemetery. The number is decreasing, but the presence remains. Actor John Gilbert, whose career would end with the arrival of sound, once wrote: "He was a prince of gallantry, and beyond all his many other attributes of artistry, comeliness and charm, a gift of royal bearing lent glamour to his being, which made him the hero lover of all time."

Soon after Valentino's death, Rambova claimed she had been receiving messages from him. In 1963, thirty-seven years after his death, actress Jane Mansfield created quite a sensation when she revealed that she had been receiving useful advice from Valentino at séances held in Falcon Lair.

Eventually both Villa Valentino and Falcon Lair were sold; Villa Valentino went to a real estate executive. When it was resold in 1951 to another realtor for three thousand dollars, it was estimated that one-and-a-half times that amount would be required to restore it to its former beauty. The house fell to "progress" before that could happen.

In 1922, this duplex became as infamous as the Brentwood house where Sharon Tate and her friends were murdered by Charles Manson and his followers in 1969. It was the scene of the murder of the director William Desmond Taylor, and the killer was never caught. But the scandal that followed revelations of studio and police cover-ups and the suspicion that the murder was linked to a love affair with a major underage star was one of the greatest in Hollywood's history.

The Year Hollywood Nearly Died—1922

Of all the years in Hollywood's century, the worst was 1922, when the film capital and its residents were beleaguered by constant criticism of the prurient nature of some of its output and the outrageous behavior of several of its leading stars. But the solution, a censor who, in the opinion of many, strangled the industry's creativity for a generation, didn't stop the public's appetite for the scandals either.

Actors misbehave, and actors frequently mistreat themselves, as a casual look at the average age of their deaths will attest. But the controversy was also inflamed by a moral climate still largely influenced by Victorian strictures and the power of institutionalized religion.

Typical of the pulpit attacks on Hollywood was that led by a conservative populist Methodist preacher named Bob Schuler, who as the first radio evangelist, easily swayed thousands. Even Tarzan's creator, Edgar Rice Burroughs, whose bills were largely paid by Hollywood, weighed in with *The Girl From Hollywood* (1923), a violent indictment of what he saw as a sex- and drug-crazed film colony.

Hollywood provided three—actually four—headline-grabbing scandals within a two-year period in the early 1920s that were among the most notorious in the entire history of Hollywood. They gave the government the perfect excuse to step in and establish a watchdog (*censor* would be the more accurate term) to make and enforce rules governing the content of movies. It was known as the Hays Office after Will Hays, President Harding's diminutive, jug-eared postmaster general, who was brought to Hollywood in 1922 by the film industry as, besieged by criticism, it tried to reform itself. The Hays Office and its successor would turn out to be the bane of filmmakers until the mid-1950s.

Many of the new rules were an overreaction to the problem: too much sex and nudity in films and too much sexual license and abuse of liquor and drugs in the film community. But then again, Hollywood, like the nation as a whole, was—on paper anyway—a very uptight community. Until Clark Gable risked a fine of several thousand dollars for uttering the final line in *Gone With the Wind* (1939), even the word *damn* couldn't be uttered in a movie. And for years, married couples always slept in separate beds—at least in the movies.

The irony is that none of the new rules governing filmmaking could have prevented the scandals, which were provoked by the misbehavior of a few actors. Like the kidnapping of the Lindbergh baby several years later, each was exploited by a sensation-seeking press, and each destroyed many of the people involved. One scandal nearly destroyed the credibility of the Los Angeles Police Force and, decades later, probably destroyed a former LA district attorney.

By March 1920, there was hardly anyone in the world—that part of it where films were shown, anyway—who didn't know who Douglas Fairbanks and Mary Pickford were; they were among the most popular actors in early films. That month the world learned that they were also lovers, when Mary filed for divorce from her first husband. Some of Mary's fame—she was known by all as "America's Sweetheart"—extended to her younger brother Jack as well. Like Mary, there was little he could do that wasn't reported to a captivated public. So when he married Olive Thomas in 1917 (like Marion Davies a former Ziegfeld chorus girl turned film star), the world noticed.

It was perfect: Jack, the handsome boy-next-door, and Olive, said to be the most beautiful woman in the world. Then on September 10, 1920, five and a half months after her in-laws married in the most publicized wedding of the era, she poisoned herself in her hotel room in Paris where she had traveled ahead of Jack to celebrate a second honeymoon. The scandal stunned millions. Apparently Olive had a taste for both heroin and a shadowy underworld life. And Jack, Mr. All-American, not only used drugs, but was cheating on his new wife. The French police attributed her suicide to depression over the marriage.

Then things got worse, much worse.

In the 1920s, much of Los Angeles was housed in what had become known as a bungalow court. To those thousands—plus the millions who dreamed of escaping to the Southern California sunshine one day—it defined the Hollywood lifestyle as clearly, if not as glamorously, as the extravagant mansions of the stars. Small, inexpensive, a single story usually designed in a U shape around a central courtyard, the bungalow court allowed privacy as well as neighborliness for those so inclined. This particularly appealed to the many lonely new arrivals hoping to break into the new industry and to those retirees who came to California, as many do to Florida today, to spend their last years in the sun. Most of the bungalows were built nearer downtown than is fashionable today, and many remain, housing newly arrived immigrants to America's most ethnically varied city.

Because it was designed with two-story, semidetached units, one such bungalow court apartment, at 404½ South Alvarado Street in the Westlake district of Los Angeles, was considered grander than most. Thus it was a popular address for successful actors like Douglas MacLean and, in bungalow B, William Desmond Taylor, who at forty-five was then one of the film community's most famous directors. The building is long gone, razed in 1966 for discount stores, and both MacLean and Taylor are largely forgotten today. But on February 1, 1922, the apartment was the site and Taylor the victim of one of Hollywood's most sensational—and still unsolved—murders, a classic crime that reads like fiction. The scandal that exploded as revelations connected the crime to some of the film industry's most celebrated actors, the studio system itself, and the Los Angeles Police Department would shock as well as titillate a nation.

William Desmond Taylor had very quickly made a name for himself as a director. His British dress and demeanor were particularly appealing to the movers and shakers of the young film industry, eager to add respectability to their financial success. But Taylor himself was as fake as a movie set. After he was found shot to death in the living room of his apartment, the *New York Times* reported that his real name was William Deanne-Tanner and that he was originally a New York actor who gave up the stage to run a shop on Fifth Avenue specializing in English antiques. He dropped out of sight in 1912. Before surfacing in Hollywood in the mid-teens and rising like a comet to the top of his newly adopted profession, Tanner worked as a hotel manager in Colorado, prospected for gold in the Yukon, and returned briefly to the stage in San Francisco.

At the time of his death it was common knowledge that Taylor was carrying on a romance with Mary Miles Minter who, although only twenty, was already a famous star billed as "the New Mary Pickford" because of her adorable little-girl looks. But as the details of his life emerged, it was discovered that he was also carrying on an affair with the actress Mabel Normand, who for years had been the great silent comedy director Mack Sennett's biggest star and lover. It was also rumored that Taylor may have been romancing Minter's dragon lady of a mother, Charlotte Shelby, as well.

Taylor's body was discovered by his butler and chauffeur, a black man named Henry Peavy, who, before calling the police, had alerted Taylor's studio, Paramount. When the homicide detectives finally got to the bungalow, they found Taylor dead, face up on the living room rug, Peavy washing dishes, and a houseful of people, including Normand and various studio executives, going through Taylor's possessions. Normand, discovered emptying drawers in the bedroom, admitted that she was looking for some letters and telegrams she had sent Taylor, but hadn't found them.

Love letters from Minter, however, were certainly found by someone; they ended up being reprinted in the press across America. Most infamously, as far as the newspapers were concerned, the police also found a collection of female lingerie in Taylor's bedroom closet, among which was a silk nightgown with the initials M.M.M. embroidered on it. A handkerchief was also found beside the body and was placed on the desk; it later disappeared.

Somewhere along the line, a doctor—or so he styled himself—arrived and, failing to turn over the victim and spot the fatal bullet wound in his back, diagnosed the cause of death as a stomach hemorrhage. He then disappeared and was never seen again, nor was the unidentified man who was seen lugging a case of bootleg scotch out the front door. Minter didn't help things much by becoming hysterical in the midst of all this (she later fainted at Taylor's funeral before a crowd of ten thousand).

Motives? They were all over the place, or seemed to be, but robbery certainly wasn't once of them. Taylor was wearing a two-thousand-dollar platinum watch and had seventy-eight dollars in the pocket of his expensive suit. Peavy was gay and, on the very day Taylor's body was found, was scheduled to appear in court for a hearing stemming from an arrest on an earlier morals charge (Taylor was to testify on his behalf). He was suspected for a while, but that soon proved a dead-end street. Peavy moved away soon thereafter, later claiming that he had been silenced by authorities and told to get out of town.

Was it blackmail? Despite the bevy of girls, there were those who suspected that Taylor himself may have been gay. Were drugs the reason? Soon after the murder it was discovered that Taylor had withdrawn thousands of dollars on the day of his murder and redeposited it. Then it was discovered that both Minter and Normand had paid him a visit on the night of the murder, with Minter apparently the last person who saw him alive. Was Taylor a drug supplier on the side?

Added to all this speculation was the discovery that Taylor's former secretary, Edward Sands, may actually have been his brother, Dennis. Sands had been fired by Taylor several months before the murder for forging checks and had departed, taking some of Taylor's money, jewelry, and one of the director's cars (Peavy had replaced him). And then there was a neighbor's story of hearing a shot about 8 P.M. on the evening before the murder and seeing a man (who may have been a woman) in a long overcoat and muffler leave Taylor's apartment about the same time. The coroner determined that Taylor had been shot with a .38-caliber, snub-nosed revolver. Based on the bullet found in Taylor's body, he concluded that it was probably a Smith and Wesson "blue break-top revolver," a small gun that could fit easily in a woman's purse.

But, as director King Vidor and others later interested in the case would discover, the probable scenario was right out of an episode of TV's *Twilight Zone*. Apparently, Minter's grandmother, Julia Miles, took a gun—some gun—back to Louisiana when she returned home after the scandal and threw it in a bayou. Some years later a new Los Angeles district attorney, Buron Fitts, tracked the gun down and presumably retrieved it. But although he apparently then had all the evidence needed to arrest Miles for the old murder, he not only failed to do that but also destroyed all the LAPD records linking her to the crime. Fitts, like his predecessor, was probably on the take from Miles.

No arrest was ever made (nor was the murder weapon found), but the brouhaha destroyed the career of Minter (who died in a little house in Santa Monica in 1984); and when it came out that Normand was addicted to drugs and Taylor may have been her dealer, her career also went into a tailspin. Despite support from her friend Mary Pickford, Normand's career was over by 1924 when her chauffeur shot Chaplin star Edna Purviance's boyfriend with a gun belonging to Normand. She died in 1930 of tuberculosis.

Then, in the early 1970s, Buron Fitts, who had served as lieutenant governor of California, committed suicide. The method? He shot himself with an old Smith and Wesson blue break-top revolver, identical to the one that police suspected had been used in the murder more than fifty years before. Truth, or the suspicion of the truth, *is* better than fiction.

The unsolved murder of William Desmond Taylor was one of the major scandals of the early 1920s that led to the creation of the Hays

Office. Another, slightly earlier and even more notorious, riveted the attention of the country as it destroyed the career of Roscoe "Fatty" Arbuckle, then a beloved film comic. The sad story proved again how prone we are to destroy the things we love the most. For Fatty Arbuckle was indeed loved by millions, second in popularity only to Charlie Chaplin (despite screenwriter Anita Loos's assertion that being fat was his only talent). When he fell, his fans turned on him with equal passion.

It all started with a Labor Day weekend party in San Francisco, only hours after Arbuckle had signed a million-dollar-a-year contract with Paramount and four months before the Taylor murder. After driving to San Francisco with two friends and various girls in his twenty-five-thousand-dollar, custom-built Pierce Arrow, Arbuckle and his entourage checked into three adjoining suites on the twelfth floor of the Palace Hotel. Liquor flowed, obtained from the best bootlegger in the city. Among the girls were Virginia Rappe, an aspiring actress ("model" was her term) who had appeared on the cover of the original sheet music for the popular song "Let Me Call You Sweetheart," and Maude Delmont, who made a specialty of providing party girls.

Two days later, Rappe was found moaning on the bed in suite 1221 and rushed to a private hospital. Delmont claimed that Arbuckle had dragged her into the room, torn her clothing off, and violently raped her (one story was that he did it with a Coca-Cola or a champagne bottle). Rappe's last words before she slipped into a coma (she died several days later, apparently of peritonitis from an unsterile abortion) accused the comic of her impending death. Arbuckle was charged with manslaughter.

There was never much of a case against him, but it made great headlines, particularly in the hands of publishing czar William Randolph Hearst. To a hypocritical public, Arbuckle was no longer the fat (close to 350 pounds), put-upon clown of films but a depraved monster. Nevertheless, two trials failed to convict him, and he was acquitted after a third in March 1922. That third jury also took the exceedingly rare step of apologizing. "We feel that a great injustice has been done to him," they stated. "Roscoe Arbuckle is entirely innocent and free from all blame."

But his career was over. Hearst's campaign ensured that many movie houses boycotted his films, and when they did run, audiences would often throw refuse at the screen. So Adolph Zukor, head of Paramount, impounded over a million dollars of unreleased Arbuckle films and, with associates like Joseph Schenck of United Artists, barred him from ever acting in movies again.

Mack Sennett had been Arbuckle's first employer in Hollywood and his frequent drinking and carousing companion and was now his safety net. Sennett kept him in funds and suggested that the former comic take up directing; he did, and under the bittersweet pseudonym of "Will B. Goode" directed a number of movies and educational films.

In 1927, six years before he died in relative obscurity in New York City, Fatty Arbuckle (as William Goodrich) directed Marion Davies, the longtime mistress of his nemesis, William Randolph Hearst, in *The Red Mill*; it would be one of the actress's favorite movies. His employer was Hearst's film company, Cosmopolitan Pictures. Hollywood irony at its most egregious.

And finally, Wallace Reid. He was a very big star by 1922. Not in the same sense that Charlie Chaplin and Douglas Fairbanks were big stars, but in his time the ruggedly handsome actor was as popular and considered as good looking as today's Tom Cruise, Tom Hanks, and Harrison Ford rolled into one. Reid played a Confederate officer in D. W. Griffith's *The Birth of a Nation* (1914), and starred opposite Metropolitan Opera star Geraldine Farrar in Cecil B. DeMille's silent version of *Carmen* (1915), among dozens of films. In many of them Reid, married to actress Dorothy Davenport and the father of two small children, played to type—an all-American family man. He also loved, and made several movies about, automobile racing.

In 1922, while filming *The World's Champion*, a boxing movie, he began forgetting lines and appeared pale and tired, unable even to stand at times. Reid publicly dismissed it as fatigue, but insiders knew better. Some time earlier Reid had been treated with cocaine by studio doctors to control the pain of an accident on the set and, as a few knew, had become seriously addicted to the drug. By 1922, it had taken control of his life, and in March his wife committed him to a private sanitarium. The following year, Wallace Reid, whom many had considered the most promising young male star of the 1920s, was dead at thirty of complications related to his drug habit. Many film histories today don't even mention him.

The year 1922 was one the film capital was glad to see end.

Mary Pickford, known from early in her career as "America's Sweetheart," was the most famous female star in the history of pictures; her husband, Douglas Fairbanks, one of the most famous male stars. When they married in 1920, the couple, soon dubbed the King and Queen of Hollywood, moved into a converted hunting lodge in Beverly Hills that they named Pickfair, and it became one of the most famous homes in the world. This photograph of the couple on Pickfair's front lawn, taken in 1924, was Pickford's favorite and, despite her divorce and remarriage, was said to be on her bedside table when she died in 1979.

America's Buckingham Palace—
Doug and Mary's Pickfair

In the 1920s and '30s, Douglas Fairbanks and Mary Pickford were the King and Queen of Hollywood, and their fairytale home—Pickfair, high atop Tower Road in Beverly Hills—was the film industry's Buckingham Palace.

Although fairly nondescript architecturally, Pickfair was the world's most glittering gathering place, easily eclipsing the White House in glamour. Not only was an invitation to Pickfair the highest symbol of success in the film colony, it was also Hollywood's most important souvenir for visiting celebrities from around the world. Among many famous guests were the Lord and Lady Louis Mountbatten (he was the present Prince Charles's uncle and the last viceroy of India, assassinated by IRA terrorists in 1978). Once a secretary from Santa Monica showed up as a self-styled Russian princess and stayed a week. In the 1920s, when humorist Will Rogers was the unofficial mayor of Beverly

Hills, he once quipped, "My most important duty as mayor is directing folks to Mary Pickford's house."

And Mary, at least, was treated like royalty (Doug was a bit too rowdy). On several occasions when she arrived late for lunch at a woman's club she belonged to, the entire group—most of them rival actresses—rose to their feet when she entered. And despite having a slightly naughty sense of humor, she could behave as stuffily as modern royalty too. In an era when Hollywood was whooping it up, Pickfair was a bastion of middle-class virtues.

Pickfair's roots went back to the early days of film, when it had been built as a hunting lodge. Fairbanks acquired it in 1919, a decade after he built Grayhall, a thirty-six-room mansion (later owned by actor George Hamilton) just west of the then somewhat remote suburb of Beverly Hills.

Fairbanks's and Pickford's roots also went back to the beginnings of film, quite literally in Mary's case. She was born Gladys Marie Smith in Toronto on—according to Pickford—April 8, 1893, (although some biographers assert it was 1892), the very year Thomas Edison patented the film projection system that would launch the movie industry.

Her father, Jack, was a clerk who died when Mary was four, leaving her mother, Charlotte, to keep herself and three children afloat by taking in sewing and roomers. Among those roomers were a pair of actors who, struck by the little girl's charm, offered her a role in a melodrama being performed by a local stock company. After that first fifty-cents-a-week job, Mary never looked back. Even education was secondary to a stage career. She taught herself arithmetic, for example, in the most practical way possible: by figuring out how much money she could save by demanding the maximum amount she could make and then spending the minimum amount possible to live. The lesson stayed with Pickford all her life, gaining the actress a reputation as one of Hollywood's shrewdest and toughest negotiators (especially if her own income was at stake) as well as one of its tightest spendthrifts. In the 1930s, when she spent a small fortune on a Rolls Royce chosen only for its "daintiness," Mary would often ask guests to bring their own steaks to barbecue at Pickfair on cook's night out.

After a decade of touring with small companies in many now legendary melodramas (including *Uncle Tom's Cabin* and *East Lynne*), Mary, by now fourteen, was "discovered" by Broadway showman David Belasco and made her Broadway debut in *The Warrens of Virginia*, a Civil War drama by William De Mille; the cast also included his younger brother, Cecil. The play was a huge success and toured the country for a year, during which both Mary and Cecil visited Los Angeles for the first time (neither liked it much). After the play closed there was very little money left over, and Charlotte suggested that Mary try movies, then filmed mostly in New York and its environs. So one day in the summer of 1909, Mary took a streetcar to the Biograph Studio on East Fourteenth Street, then the best movie production company in the fledgling industry, and talked the company's chief director, D. W. Griffith, into hiring her. Not only did he hire her, he took her on for ten dollars a day, double the going rate.

Although the diminutive Pickford played children in the first two films of the seventy-nine she made for Griffith in the following year and a half (such was the production standard of the industry at the time), she was usually cast as characters nearer her own age, sixteen or seventeen. Thereafter, as long as she worked in films, she was typecast as an adorable curly haired adolescent. She soon moved to California and commenced making films for Famous Players (later Paramount Pictures).

But long before she made her most famous film, *Rebecca of Sunnybrook Farm* (1917), and getting the industry's first million-dollar contract, Pickford was already referred to by the nickname Sid Graumann's father coined to promote the San Francisco opening of *Tess of the Storm Country* (1914). Then and forever, she would be known to her adoring public as "America's Sweetheart."

Douglas Ulman (Fairbanks's original name) was born in Denver, Colorado, on May 23, 1883, and like Mary started acting at an early age. His father was a Shakespearian scholar, and young Doug could recite entire plays by the Bard by the time he was twelve. Nevertheless, it was only after he graduated from Denver's East High School that he decided acting and not engineering would be his career. And despite a couple of lapses (including an early marriage when he sold soap for his father-in-law's company), he, like Mary, was an actor all his life.

Fairbanks was a natural for the stage and—because he possessed what was probably the biggest smile in the theater and a predilection for breathtaking acrobatic hijinks—film, too. In fact, it was D. W. Griffith himself who suggested that the young actor get into films after seeing him vault a hedge in New York's Central Park in 1914. So it wasn't too surprising that Griffith's Triangle Films (founded by the then big three of filmmakers—Thomas Ince, D. W. Griffith, and Mack Sennett—to compete with Famous Players) offered him two thousand dollars a week and, since that was more or less a king's ransom in those days, equally unsurprising that he took it. By the fall of the next year, 1916, Fairbanks (who, like his mother, had assumed the surname of an earlier husband of his mother, Ella, because it sounded more genteel [and Gentile] than "Ulman") was one of the most famous stars in America, second only to Charlie Chaplin—and Mary Pickford.

He was also an ardent lady's man, so when he met Pickford, unhappily married to an actor named Owen Moore ("the Beau Brummell of Biograph," Mary once called him), at a party in New York's Westchester County, it wasn't long before the couple were seriously involved. Because they were both highly visible celebrities, soon tongues started wagging. The couple's clandestine romance (carried on in part during a hugely successful tour with Charlie Chaplin to sell Liberty Bonds after America entered the war), divorces, and marriage on March 28, 1920, inspired an early example of the no-holds-barred celebrity journalism we know so well today. Although the couple tried to keep their romance quiet, even donning disguises to render them less recognizable when they met privately, they were very public in planning a project that would shake Hollywood's studio system to its roots.

In January 1919, Mary and Doug (as they were then called by everybody), along with Chaplin and D. W. Griffith, formed the industry's first independent production and distribution company. They named it United Artists, and although greatly changed in its operations, it's still with us today. UA was successful from the start, despite naysayers like journalist Richard Rowland, whose famous quip greeted Fairbanks's announcement of the new company: "The lunatics have taken over the asylum."

The couple's films, particularly those made at their own Fairbanks-Pickford production studio on Santa Monica Boulevard and distributed through United Artists, couldn't have been more successful. From their studio, isolated from the nitty gritty of the workplace in private, fully staffed bungalows and a professionally equipped gymnasium complete with a Turkish bath for Doug, the couple turned out many of the era's landmark film successes. They included Doug's *The Three Musketeers*, *The Thief of Bagdad*, and *Zorro*, and Mary's *Pollyanna* and *Little Lord Fauntleroy*. In *Fauntleroy*, incidentally, the twenty-eight-year-old Pickford played both the golden-haired male child Fauntleroy and his mother, Dearest, a compromise between her fans' demands and her own desire to play a woman on screen.

There, too, Fairbanks made one of his most definitive films, *Douglas Fairbanks in Robin Hood*, billed that way to stop the competition from capitalizing on his fame by rushing other Robin Hoods into production. Made in October 1922, it was the biggest production Hollywood had ever seen, twice as expensive as Griffith's *Intolerance*, and it received the biggest publicity send-off of any film until *Gone With the Wind* was released seventeen years later. It was described as the most expensive film ever made (at $750,000 it was, but it didn't cost a million dollars, as publicized) and was made in a copy of a Norman castle, itself publicized as bigger than anything like it in England (not true; although it was large, it wasn't much bigger than an airplane hangar).

When, four years later Fairbanks's film *The Black Pirate* opened on a double bill with Pickford's *Sparrows* at Graumann's Egyptian Theater an interesting facet of Pickford's business judgment (which would make her one of the richest women in the world) was demonstrated. Regardless of their fans' clamor, the couple never made a complete film together until the twilight of their film careers. That film was *The Taming of the Shrew* (1929), the first sound film of a Shakespeare play. The reason, according to Mary, was economic—two films bring in more money than one—and her fear that, however much she longed for adult roles, the romantic scenario implicit in making a film together would compromise her little-girl image and the box-office receipts.

When they married, Fairbanks had already moved from Grayhall into the house that would soon be named Pickfair. Purchased by Fairbanks for $37,261.77, the six-room house, originally a hunting lodge and located on an eighteen-acre lot on the highest point of land above the growing community of Beverly Hills, was quickly remodeled into a five-bedroom mansion. New amenities included sleeping porches (essential in those days before air-conditioning), a kidney-shaped, Olympic-sized swimming pool (the first private swimming pool in Beverly Hills, its cabanas were stocked with swimming suits fitting all sizes from "teeny tots to fatsos"), blue-and-white marble floors in the halls, a dormitory for the staff of fifteen servants, and a cottage for the majordomo, Albert. Behind the house there were kennels housing, among other pets, Fairbanks's German shepherd and Mary's wire-haired terrier (Zorro), stables for horses and the two cows that provided morning milk for the couple and their guests, a tennis court, and a miniature golf course. Pickfair's commanding views, stretching from ocean to mountains, prompted other silent film stars to leave the traffic of Hollywood for the wide open spaces of Beverly Hills.

Pickfair's interior, even after an early 1930s remodeling to give the place a new look for the many international celebrities expected to make the pilgrimage to the top of Tower Road during the 1932 Olympics, was a bit of a mishmash, albeit an expensive one. One visitor categorized the result, designed by Elsie de Wolfe, as "Waldorf-Astoria French Empire." An exception was a room filled with Oriental knickknacks collected by the couple during their Far Eastern travels, where guests were served cocktails by servants dressed in Kabuki-style costumes.

The gilt-and-ivory living room, where meetings took place that would result in the formation in 1929 of the Academy of Motion Picture Arts and Sciences, was filled with authentic Louis XVI furniture and rare Aubusson rugs. The set of china Napoleon gave Josephine on their wedding day was displayed in a cabinet.

Pickford usually received guests in the adjoining sunroom from which she also (with Joseph Schenck) ran United Artists. Mary's bedroom was lavender and green, Doug's brown, and another, always reserved for Charlie Chaplin (who often slept over even though his house was only a block away) was rose. Another room was decorated as an Old West saloon, filled with Doug's collection of Western memorabilia, including several paintings by Charles Russell and Frederick Remington, and fitted with a huge mahogany bar that was built in Europe and shipped around Cape Horn in 1854 for a saloon in Auburn, California. The bar was Mary's Christmas present to Doug in 1931, intended as the basis of his planned Western museum.

Dinner at Pickfair was always a formal, multiple-course affair served precisely at 7 P.M., and because Doug had a habit of spontaneously inviting people for dinner, the table (which could accommodate three dozen guests) was always set for fifteen. An eclectic mixture of people gathered around that table, from visiting royalty to Henry and Clara Ford, to prizefighter Bull Montana (Fairbanks's sparring partner when Gene Tunny or Jack Dempsey weren't around), to directors like Alan Dwan and Howard Hawks, who became expert at playing a game they named "Doug"—a strenuous form of the then-popular badminton, played with a high net and heavy, lead-loaded shuttlecocks on Pickfair's tennis court. On one memorable evening, Albert Einstein attempted explaining his theory of relativity by pushing his silverware and plates around the table.

Plagued by indigestion, Mary ate only spinach and milk when working on a film. After dinner she had a French lesson before joining Doug and their guests to watch a movie in the living room, where a screen was built into a wall. Because Doug and Mary arose at 5 A.M. when they were working, Albert would pass around cups of Ovaltine at 11 P.M., and everyone went home.

Certainly one reason for Doug and Mary's popularity was their apparent willingness to share their private lives—or what seemed to be their private lives—with their fans. Everyone knew that Doug wouldn't let Mary bob her hair in the style of the era (and she didn't for years), that he wouldn't let her wear short skirts, and that they called each other by more than fifty pet names. Fans also knew that, because of his intense jealousy, Doug wouldn't let Mary dance with anyone but himself, which nearly led to an international incident during a visit to England, when she refused to waltz with a charming man with a slight stutter at a high-society ball; he was the duke of York, later George VI, king of England, emperor of India, and the father of Queen Elizabeth II.

As far as anyone knows, the couple never exchanged a cross or impatient word with the press, even allowing photographers to shoot

Mary making coffee over a campfire in the course of a walk and handing Doug a brick when he built a wall at Pickfair. Obviously much of this was a little forced (including a well-known, obviously posed, but nevertheless naively sweet shot of the couple in a canoe floating in their swimming pool). But they actually seemed not to mind it all (or the impact on their box-office receipts).

But all good things must end. Mary's mother, Charlotte, to whom she was devoted, died in 1928. That year Mary finally cut off her curls, bobbed her hair, and made a few movies that did her reputation little good (in particular her first film with Fairbanks, *The Gaucho*, which happened to be his worst, in which she played a cameo as the Virgin Mary). Doug was getting restless too, and his breathtaking athleticism, always better than his acting, was beginning to suffer. Perhaps he was experiencing a midlife crisis in his marriage and career—both had been subjected to the full glare of publicity for more than a decade. Or he might have simply had cabin fever. Part of the problem with Pickfair, despite its air of success and glamour, was that it could be a gilded prison. "I want to go places," he said in 1930. And so he did, sometimes traveling with Mary but mostly without, exploring remote places like Manchuria, Cambodia, and French Indochina (now Vietnam), as well as more familiar destinations like Japan and the Philippines. Before long he was returning to Pickfair only for Christmas and special occasions.

Mary too was having problems of a nature guaranteed to get her attention; her box office was dropping. "A grown-up Ma——alas, perhaps too well grown," wrote the *New York Times*, "has taken the place of what seemed inexhaustible youth incarnate." Even without the golden curls, it wasn't easy for Pickford, famed for her adorable little-girl persona, to compete in a sound and Technicolor world populated by such seductive sirens as Garbo, Harlow, and Swanson. So Mary, like many stars before and since, started filling her days by laying endless cornerstones and accepting honors (she was the first female Grand Marshal of the Rose Parade in 1933). She also toyed with a return to Broadway.

On July 3, 1933, Pickford announced her separation from Doug, in

London at the time, and apologized to her fans for "ruining their Fourth of July holiday." Soon the powerful Hearst gossip columnist Louella Parsons revealed that Mary had been seeing an actor-bandleader named Charles ("Buddy") Rogers and that Doug was seeing Lady Sylvia Ashley (later to be Clark Gable's fourth wife).

The fairy tale all America once wanted to believe in ended with the couple's divorce on January 10, 1935. Fairbanks married Sylvia six weeks later. Mary and Buddy married in June 1937, and the reception for three hundred industry leaders (including the Cecil B. DeMilles and the Samuel Goldwyns) was held at Pickfair. Doug and Sylvia, vacationing in Santa Monica only a few miles away, were not invited nor did they send congratulations.

On Monday, December 12, 1939, while living in the Santa Monica beach house where he and Sylvia had decided to sit out the war, Doug complained of chest pains. Awaking at midnight, he asked that the window be opened so he could hear the surf, grinning as he assured an attending nurse that he had "never felt better." Within minutes he died of a massive coronary. He was only fifty-six. "He was make-believe at it best," said the *New York Times*. "He was a complete fantasy . . . unabashed and joyous. He seemed to go through life leaping balustrades, scaling walls, and beaming his never-to-be-forgotten 'million-dollar smile.'"

Mary, ever more reclusive, ever more conservative, lived on at Pickfair until her death forty years later in May 1979, watched over and guarded by the loyal Rodgers. After her death, the estate was sold for $5,362,500 to Los Angeles sports magnate Jerry Buss. Entrepreneur Mishulam Riklis and his wife, actress Pia Zadora, bought it in 1987 for seven million dollars. Although they largely demolished the legendary house (but kept the pool), what they replaced it with was basically an eleven-million-dollar, modernized version of the original.

Douglas Fairbanks Jr., Fairbanks's son by his first wife, Beth Sully, and a renowned actor in his own right, was one of the first guests invited to tour the rebuilt Pickfair. "It's no longer a hunting lodge; now it's a mansion," he said.

And of course, it's no longer Pickfair.

Before the challenge of television, the arrival of sound in 1928 created the biggest upheaval in Hollywood's filmmaking century. Countless new jobs were created, as studios had to rebuild or remodel what would be called sound-stages, and film laboratories had to reequip their entire operations, but equally many jobs (like title writers) evaporated overnight. Actors were especially vulnerable. The career of Greta Garbo, seen here with her costar and real-life lover John Gilbert in the silent film *Love* (1927), soared on sound (her 1930 film, *Anna Christie*, was promoted by ads trumpeting "Garbo Talks!"). Gilbert's career, however, was instantly destroyed; his voice recorded badly, and sound drew attention to his hammy acting.

"You Ain't Heard Nothin' Yet"— Sound Arrives

When the advertisements proclaimed "Garbo talks!" for the premiere of Greta Garbo's first sound movie, *Anna Christie* (1930), people flocked to see and at last to hear the Swedish beauty. The words she first, famously, spoke in her guttural accent, "Gimme a visky," have become as famous in Hollywood lore as those spoken by singer Al Jolson in *The Jazz Singer,* somewhat incorrectly credited with being the first "talkie," two years before: "You ain't heard nothin' yet." With the arrival of sound, not only did the silent era disappear, but so did an entire way of storytelling in Hollywood, and with it thousands of careers. What replaced them may have seemed more up to date but not, in the opinion of many, better.

Actually, there was no "first" talkie in the 1920s. Although the fact is little known, sound had been around from the movie industry's infancy in 1901, when a German physics professor named Reuhmer first recorded sound waves on film. Five years later a French inventor,

Eugene Lauste, patented a system of recording sound using an arc and vibrating wires. In 1907, a friend of Lauste's son named Arthur Kingston went to work for a Paris firm, Matelot et Gentilhomme, that was already making talking films for Pathé by having actors mime action in synchronization with a prerecorded disk, which was then amplified to fill an auditorium. Two years later, long before electronic sound arrived in the 1920s, Kingston was *already* making electric recordings. So far the legend that Thomas Edison's assistant W. K. L. Dickson made a film of himself talking in 1889 remains just that: a legend.

As astonishing as it may appear from today's perspective in which a movie's sound—the score, sound effects, dialogue, and so on—is considered nearly as important to a film's success as its visuals, no one then thought sound was of much consequence. Not only was it thought unimportant, it was actually considered highly threatening to the integrity of film as an art form.

"We talk," wrote James Quirk in *Photoplay* in the mid-1920s, "of the worth, service, the entertaining power, the community value, the recreative force, the educational influence, the civilizing and commercial possibilities of the motion picture. And everyone has . . . neglected to mention its rarest and subtlest beauty: silence."

Quirk argued that the greatest processes in the universe are silent, and therefore the greatest arts must be the silent ones. "The value of silence in art is its stimulation to the imagination, and the imaginative quality is art's highest appeal. The really excellent motion pictures [are] never mere photography. Continually they cause the beholder to hear things which they suggest—the murmurs of a summer night, the pounding of the surf, the sigh of the wind in the trees, the babel of crowded streets, the whisperings of love. The talking picture will be made practical, but it will never supercede the motion picture without sound. It will lack the subtlety and suggestion of vision—that vision which, deprived of voice, to ears of flesh, intones undisturbed symphonies of the soul."

It was an opinion vigorously championed by the world's most famous movie star, Charlie Chaplin. More than the tremendous cost of converting moviemaking to sound (about which more later), film, as far as Chaplin, Quirk, and virtually the entire film establishment of the era were concerned, was a *mime* art. Adding sound changed it profoundly to a *theatrical* art. The arrival of sound would certainly curtail Chaplin's work. After grudgingly giving into it with *Modern Times* (1936) nearly a decade after sound was introduced (and then only using it for one song) and misusing it in *The Great Dictator* (1940) in an embarrassing, sermonizing ending, he made only four pictures in the next thirty years.

Silent films were doing fine commercially. In fact, many of the greatest of the silent films, including MGM's *Ben-Hur* and the French director Abel Gance's *Napoleon,* were made at the very end of the silent era.

Then the industry hit a slump and needed a novelty. According to film historian Kevin Brownlow, radio had by then attuned the public to the sound of canned dialogue, and, as television would do a generation later, it was the dedication of the public to the newfangled entertainment medium that kept them away from run-of-the-mill movies, resulting in the box-office downturn.

Movie sound was, of course, the novelty—specifically via the Warner Brothers–owned Vitaphone system, a refinement of the synchronized sound-on-disk system. Warner Brothers, still clinging to the old prejudices, never planned to use the Vitaphone system for voice but only for music and effects like thunder or cannon shots. When their first production, *Vitaphone Prelude*, debuted on August 6, 1926, aside from a spoken introduction by Will Hays, Hollywood's morals censor, that's all there was. In retrospect the problems with sound on disks seem obvious, but the industry was learning a new technology. Two weeks after the opening, a Western Electric engineer was in the audience and reported that when Hays opened his mouth, the twanging sounds of a banjo came out. And the unintended humor caused when the needle stuck in the record groove as the action continued was notorious.

A year later, Warner Brothers stunned Hollywood with the movie that convinced the industry that, like it or loathe it, sound was here to stay. The movie was a sentimental story of a young man who prefers singing modern music instead of the music of his Jewish heritage called *The Jazz Singer*. It starred the hugely popular stage entertainer Al Jolson. There would be no spoken dialogue—only his singing of six songs. But Jolson deliberately ad-libbed extensively when the disks were turning, and Warner decided to leave the comments in. Ergo the famous line, "You ain't heard nothin' yet!"

Despite a few negative reviews (*Photoplay* again), the audiences went crazy with excitement when the movie premiered on October 6, 1927. A year later there were sixteen soundstages in Hollywood, and theaters all across the country were being wired for sound. By April 1929, sixteen hundred theaters had been converted. About this time Western Electric introduced a sound-on-film system that it had been working on for more than a decade, and the future was clear. Still, for years many sound-equipped theaters maintained both systems and Hollywood released films in both sound and silent versions for the theaters that hadn't made the conversion. Technicolor was being thrown into films here and there also, a notable example being the scene with Mary and the Christ child in MGM's *Ben-Hur*, made as a silent film in 1926 and remade, none too successfully, as a sound picture in 1931.

Many have said that it was a pity the changeover from silent film to sound didn't take a little longer, thus softening the economic blow as well as allowing the new art to find its way (early talkies were verbose to a fault, often drowning action with dialogue). But as Hollywood historian Kevin Brownlow put it: ". . . everything was ruled by King Mike."

Although many new jobs were created in the industry when sound arrived, untold numbers of employees saw their jobs evaporate overnight. Musicians were hard hit (until the industry needed them to record music for sound films), laboratories had to completely reequip their operations, title writers became as obsolete as the dodo bird, and directors—unless they had stage (i.e., theatrical) experience—went begging. But the worst hit in terms of visibility were the actors, many of them major stars.

Clara Bow, dubbed "the It girl" by English writer Elinor Glyn, was finished by 1930. It wasn't entirely her voice that did her in at the age of only twenty-five (after forty-eight films), although her high-pitched instrument wasn't exactly what people anticipated from a sex siren. The killer was the clumsy, heavy, early sound equipment that restricted Bow's usual cavorting around the set, which had created an impression of carefree freedom that audiences adored. (Details of her fairly lurid private life became public about the same time, severely damaging her career as well.)

Other new jobs were created. To avoid losing its huge foreign market, Hollywood had to find a way to solve the problem of selling sound films in non-English-speaking markets, by then a huge financial consideration. The first solutions were clumsy: For the German version of *Anna Christie,* the entire film was reshot. Greta Garbo could, of course, repeat her role in German, but the balance of the cast was completely replaced. Antonio Moreno remade several of John Barrymore's films for the Spanish-speaking market (directed by Ramon Novarro, a Mexican, who after Rudolph Valentino's death in 1926 replaced him as Hollywood's sexy Latin Lover).

Nonindustry jobs materialized too. To fill the needs of sound, Hollywood immediately started to tap the Broadway stage. Then it was discovered that there were too few apartments in Hollywood to house the new arrivals. Cecil B. DeMille, who also dabbled in real estate, solved the problem by buildings at least one of many now-famous Spanish revival apartment buildings, complete with courtyards and fountains. His is the Villa DeMille (originally the El Cabrillo), designed by the Zwebells, at the corner of Franklin and Grace Avenues. Now restored to its former glory, it has reputedly housed actors from Greta Garbo to Stevie Wonder.

One celebrated career ended by the advent of sound was also one of the most notorious as it involved rumors of revenge by the film capital's most powerful studio chief, Louis B. Mayer. Although his name is largely unknown to most moviegoers today, John Gilbert—Jack, as he was known to everyone—was one of Hollywood's most famous leading men in the 1920s.

After making a number of unimpressive films for Fox, Gilbert signed with MGM in 1924 where his real potential was realized in such films as King Vidor's *The Big Parade* (1925) and Erich von Stroheims's *The Merry Widow,* made the following year. The same year he also starred opposite Greta Garbo (with whom he was carrying on a highly publicized love affair) in the sensationally popular *Flesh and the Devil.* Then sound arrived, and it destroyed him.

At least that is the legend. The fact is that Gilbert had always been more of a ham than an actor, miming his way through silents. When sound arrived, changing filmmaking to a theatrical discipline, he was lost. By 1929, Louis B. Mayer was nearing his fill of Gilbert's less-than-stellar talent, alcoholism, womanizing, and professional capriciousness. To introduce his leading man in talkies, Mayer chose a script called *Redemption*, adapted from a Tolstoy novel, *The Living Corpse*. Then, not too helpfully, Mayer chose Lionel Barrymore to direct it, despite the well-known fact that Barrymore was by then addicted to morphine, which he had begun using to counteract the constant pain of arthritis.

Gossip claimed that Mayer deliberately set out to destroy Gilbert by selecting Barrymore, but this doesn't fly. When Mayer discovered that Barrymore could do nothing with Gilbert (his sound acting was melodramatic, complete with rolled r's), Barrymore was replaced with the respected Fred Niblo, who was unable to do much more. Because the public was demanding to hear Gilbert speak, however, the actor was immediately rushed into a second picture (also directed by Barrymore) called *His Glorious Night*. It was one of the biggest mistakes of Mayer's career.

Finished in only thirteen days to satisfy the demands of MGM exhibitors, *His Glorious Night* was laughed off the screen when it opened and Gilbert squeaked the words, "I love you! I love you!"

Many have accused Mayer of deliberately sabotaging the sound track to destroy Gilbert. That makes no sense, since not only did Mayer have a lot of money invested in the movie and his star, but he had the release of Gilbert's *Redemption* coming the following year. The best guess is that the problem lay with the sound-recording techniques of the time, which favored baritones (Gilbert was a tenor).

Although Gilbert made several films afterward, it was all-downhill. At one point he even took a full-page ad in *Variety* pleading for work and asserting that MGM would neither release his films nor hire him. This was not true as it turned out. Although it was at her demand, he costarred with Garbo in *Queen Christina*, an MGM production, in 1933.

John Gilbert died of a heart attack on January 9, 1936, at his Beverly Hills home. Marlene Dietrich, with whom he was romantically involved at the time, was said to have been with him that night but to have left before the ambulance arrived. He was thirty-eight. Whether Dietrich was there or not, she did make an unforgettable appearance at Gilbert's funeral by walking up the aisle in tears and then fainting dramatically. She later bought Gilbert's bedsheets for seven hundred dollars, presumably the ones on which the couple had made love.

The silent era had ended. King Mike ruled.

For the silent film generation, the Hotel Hollywood, located at the then-muddy intersection of today's Hollywood Boulevard and Highland Avenue, was the center of the movie capital's social orbit, inspiring a famous song ("The End of a Perfect Day") in 1909 and a star-studded nationwide radio show in the 1930s. Everyone stayed there, from Cecil B. DeMille (making his first film in 1913) to Greta Garbo (who registered incognito) to Gloria Swanson and Louis B. Mayer. Today its site is the location of a new multimillion-dollar theater that, beginning in 2002, will be the permanent home for the Academy Awards ceremonies. Actress Wanda Hawley poses in the drive in this 1922 shot.

Hollywood's Hotel——Heaven for Some

When Rudolph Valentino, then a struggling actor re-cently arrived from New York City, and his first wife, Jean Acker, were married on November 5, 1919, there was no question where they would spend their wedding night; it would be in her room at the Hotel Hollywood.

It was the most prestigious hotel in town, and Acker, a screenwriter making a comfortable two hundred dollars a week, already lived there. So did a lot of film luminaries far more famous than the relatively unknown Acker. Louis B. Mayer and Irving Thalberg, his wunderkind production director, shared a suite (Thalberg lived in it; Mayer lived with his family nearby). Other registered guests included Jack Warner, Wallace Reid, Gloria Swanson, Greta Garbo (who registered incognito), and Pola Negri. In fact, for many years between February 1903, when the first 33-room building (with just two baths) was built across from a strawberry field at the northwest corner of Highland and Hollywood Boulevard, and, in 1956, when the next 144-room hotel was razed, it was the social center of Hollywood. Just about everything that counted in Hollywood, starting with the town's first benefit in 1905 (which raised fifteen dollars and 203 books to establish Hollywood's first library), took place at the Hotel Hollywood, at least until the stars started moving west toward Beverly Hills about the time sound arrived in 1927. At about the same time, the hotel changed its name to Hollywood Hotel, but both names were used interchangeably during the life of the building.

Even if they didn't live there, many of the stars lived nearby. The close-knit community partied in the hotel's dining room, later christened "the Dining Room of the Stars" (where silent comedian Roscoe "Fatty" Arbuckle thought it the height of comedy to flip pats of butter to the ceiling), or danced the night away to "Alexander's Ragtime Band" or the romantic "Kiss Me Again" at the Thursday night dances in the ballroom. Sometimes when the crowds got too large, they would roll up the lobby carpets and make merry there as well.

Carrie Jacobs Bond wrote her then-famous (and still familiar) song, "The End of a Perfect Day," at the Hotel Hollywood in 1909. Five years later, opera star Geraldine Farrar was welcomed to Hollywood with the town's first white-tie-and-tails party held in the hotel's ballroom. The Hearst newspaper's famous gossip columnist Louella Parsons made the hotel's name synonymous with glamour for millions when she used it as the setting for radio-broadcast visits with film stars of the day during the 1930s.

The Hotel Hollywood also resonated on a more mundane level. In 1920, when a guest became too ill to be transported to the nearest hospital in Los Angeles, he had to be temporarily housed in a closer facility: the local insane asylum. The incident prompted the hotel's owner, Myra Hershey (of the chocolate family), to organize the community's first adult hospital. Today it's the huge Hollywood Presbyterian Medical Center.

For some of those early days, the Hotel Hollywood was hardly the elegant hostelry it would become. Mack Sennett recalls that Hollywood Boulevard (then called Prospect Avenue) was "a semi-dirt street with a little pavement in the center and a one-track trolley. When it rained, it was muddy. You had to put chains on your tires." The hotel, essentially a country resort in a rural wilderness, had to be entirely self-sufficient and so had its own power and ice plants. "On Vine Street they grew grapes," Sennett recalled in reminiscing about his early filmmaking days in Hollywood. "That's how it got its name."

When Cecil B. DeMille arrived in 1913 to make his first film, *The Squaw Man,* he and his colleagues stayed at the Hotel Hollywood. Bessie Lasky, wife of DeMille's partner Jesse Lasky, described the hotel at the time as "a dismal summer hotel, filled with unwanted summer boarders, their aged bodies looking blank and useless, rocking on the porch, filling the air with futility and gloom." She and DeMille recalled that there was only one clerk (wearing the era's ubiquitous green eye-shade, of course), who spent most of his time dozing, and a creaky elevator; their rooms were smelly and stuffy, and a bathroom faucet ran only a trickle of brown water. A month later the director rented a house nearby and moved out.

By the 1920s, however, the Hotel Hollywood had become so synonymous with the film community's high living that it had become a target for the era's tabloid journalism. "The grand old Hotel Hollywood," the fan magazine *Photoplay* captioned a picture of the hotel that showed not a trace of a human being, "film land's first and most famous inn, on a busy licentious afternoon. Note the orgy in progress on the front lawn." It was surely the greatest compliment ever paid a clump of stunted trees.

There's no question that *Photoplay* was partly correct; inevitably some "hanky-panky" (a term from the era) was going on just as in any other hotel then or now. And because of the high visibility of the stars, it made good gossip. Nevertheless, the Hotel Hollywood attempted to maintain a visage of dour respectability. When John Barrymore leaped into the room of his leading lady from the garden, the management ordered spiny cactus planted in front of all the ground-floor rooms to dissuade others from such amorous athletics. When that proved ineffective, the management ordered all ground-floor windows nailed shut.

It may not have been the same clerk who so depressed Lasky and DeMille who demanded Valentino produce a marriage license before he could go upstairs with Jean Acker after their wedding. In any event, he needn't have bothered. That night, after the Latin Lover led his bride to her room, Acker, a lesbian, slammed the door in Valentino's face, locked it, and wailed that she had made a terrible mistake. That was the end of the marriage, although the couple didn't actually divorce for three years—three years during which he would become one of the most famous male stars of the century. Later, at the peak of his fame and fortune, Valentino would remark in complete disregard for his circumstances at the time of his marriage: "Jean had always claimed that she wanted to be my soul-mate when in fact all she wanted to be was my check-mate."

Although the Hotel Hollywood began to lose its glamour when stars began moving west to Beverly Hills, and the biggest social events it hosted were the senior proms of Hollywood High School built two block's away, some images of its fame remained until the day it was torn down. The ceiling of the dining room was studded with gold stars, each bearing the name of a film great who had eaten there often (Sennett recalls that lunch cost forty-five cents). Those names included Douglas Fairbanks, Norma Shearer, Lon Chaney, and William Farnum, who came to Hollywood with DeMille in 1913 to star in the director's first movie and lived in a triple suite at the hotel.

Most of the residents, of course, weren't stars. And some lived there for years, even decades. Just before the building was demolished, writer Ezra Goodman stopped by and visited some of them. One old woman, who had lived at the hotel for thirty-five years, was dismayed at the prospect of leaving. "I don't want to go to heaven," she said, rocking on the veranda overlooking Hollywood Boulevard, by then beginning to be crowded with garish souvenir shops. "I just want to stay here."

If historic buildings have ghosts, the ghosts of those who once lived at the old Hotel Hollywood should feel good—or at least redeemed—these days. On the site of the long gone hostelry that was so central to the life of the film capital, a new theater is being built. Starting in 2002 it will be the site of the Academy Awards ceremonies, the first permanent home Oscar has had in his seventy years of life.

Marion Davies, the effervescent actress who was publishing czar William Randolph Hearst's mistress for thirty-five years, reaches for the brass ring from a carousel erected by the pool for a 1937 costume party at the couple's legendary Ocean House. Built in 1922 as the biggest and most opulent beach house in California, it boasted 110 rooms (55 were bedrooms), a marble-lined swimming pool with more than a thousand lockers for visitors, a ballroom taken from an eighteenth-century palazzo, and a dining room hung with a dozen huge portraits of Davies costumed for her most famous film roles. Today, all that remains of the house where Charlie Chaplin often did impersonations for dinner guests is a parking lot and the decaying, seven-thousand-square-foot guest wing.

Xanadu by the Sea—Marion Davies and William Randolph Hearst's Ocean House

Nearly everyone who knows something about film is aware that Orson Welles's *Citizen Kane* (1941), hailed as the greatest film ever made by many critics, was not so subtly based on the life (and lifestyle) of America's most famous and powerful press lord, William Randolph Hearst.

And nearly everyone remembers that the plot of the film is driven by the search for whoever or whatever Charles Foster Kane's last word, "Rosebud," signified. The audience knows all along that Rosebud is the name of Kane's childhood sled, more beloved by the tycoon than the riches and possessions that came later. Far fewer know that the word had a much more personal meaning for Hearst; Rosebud was his pet name for the clitoris of the woman who would be his mistress for thirty-five years, the effervescent actress and ex-Ziegfeld follies girl Marion Davies. For her Hearst created an entire film production company and an imperial lifestyle rarely matched in Hollywood. Ocean House, one of the grandest beach houses ever built in America, was built for her.

Citizen Kane was merciless to Davies as well as Hearst, portraying her as an alcoholic singer named Susan Alexander with operatic pretensions. Just in case someone missed the point, Welles even has her playing with huge jigsaw puzzles as she mopes the nights away in Xanadu, a parody of Hearst's opulent San Simeon estate atop his "Enchanted Hill" some two hundred miles up the coast from Los Angeles. Davies, as was well-known at the time, was often bored when the couple were at San Simeon and whiled away the time with jigsaw puzzles. As more than one observer has commented, it's a wonder Welles didn't have the Susan Alexander character imitate Marion Davies's well-known stammer in the movie as well.

Hearst, for all his bluster, was deeply hurt by *Citizen Kane,* less for its parody of him than for its portrayal of Alexander as an alcoholic (Davies, in fact, had a drinking problem most of her life). Davies was angered by the film, but being one of Hollywood's least mean-spirited personalities (as well as one of its most generous), she rarely showed it, even when it became clear that the movie had effectively ended her film career. It was seen by the public as validating the fairly common opinion of the time that her fame owed more to Hearst's deep pockets than her own talent.

At the time, and until the last decade of her life, she rose above the furor and gossip by escaping to Ocean House, her beach home in Santa Monica, where for a generation she hosted parties with a panache that is still legendary. Hearst especially loved costume parties, so there were plenty of those in the house that could—and occasionally did—host two thousand guests. If Mary Pickford and Douglas Fairbanks's Pickfair was Hollywood's Buckingham Palace in the 1920s and early '30s, Ocean House was its Riviera playground.

Joseph Kennedy was a frequent guest, often with Gloria Swanson on his arm. Winston Churchill and his eighteen-year-old son, Randolph, were hosted by Hearst and Davies at Ocean House in August 1929, and Randolph's memories of the event open a wonderful window on Hollywood's jazz-age aristocracy at play. He described Ocean House as "a magnificent place looking on the sea, with a wonderful marble swimming bath of great length and very well heated."

"Marion had collected a dinner party of 60 for us," Churchill continued. "The stars included Pola Negri, Charlie Chaplin, [and] Harold Lloyd. I failed to recognize either Charlie or Harold since moustache and horn-rimmed glasses were missing.

"After dinner we danced and then Marion stimulated Charlie into doing some impersonations. She did Sarah Bernhardt and Lillian Gish, and then he did Napoleon [and] John Barrymore as Hamlet and many others. He is absolutely superb and enchanted everyone. He also did some terribly complicated patter dancing, as also did Marion. She is delightfully stimulating and must have danced and frolicked around for about 1½ hours after a hard day's work."

At one point in the evening, after discovering that she and Winston Churchill shared a taste for gin, Davies led the future prime minister of Great Britain on a tour of several of Ocean House's fifty-five bathrooms where, because Hearst disapproved of her drinking, she would hide her stash of gin and Scotch in the toilet tanks. Understandably she occasionally forgot in which bathroom she had hidden it.

The Ocean House location, a prime site on Beach Palisades Road (later Pacific Coast Highway) in Santa Monica was, in those days before Malibu became the beach site of choice, home to many celebrities. Neighbors included Louis B. Mayer, Harold Lloyd, Will Rogers, Irving Thalberg (the boy wonder of MGM who would die at thirty-seven), and his wife, actress Norma Shearer.

From its inception in 1922, Ocean House was planned to be the biggest beach house in California. It was a white, Georgian-style, shingled structure—actually five buildings linked in the shape of a U. As at San Simeon, entire interiors were bought and shipped from European castles to fill many of its 110 rooms. "You could take a tour of the great houses of Europe just by walking through Ocean House," quipped one guest who visited the mansion often in its later years. The length of the pool praised by Churchill—in feet—was also 110. He neglected to note that it contained fresh water, was paneled with marble, and sported a Venetian-style bridge spanning its width. The bathing amenities included a thousand lockers for guests.

Eighteen soaring Ionic columns marched the length of the beach facade of the house, more, Chaplin once remarked, "than the Supreme Court Building in Washington." The paneling in the dining room, reception room, and drawing room, each more than sixty feet long, came from an estate in Ireland. There was also a huge ballroom taken from a mid–eighteenth century Italian palazzo, in which larger dinners were held and where every weekend an orchestra played during a buffet for upward of 150 guests. There was a real British tavern dating from 1560 that seated fifty and had a dance floor and an ice cream fountain for children. And until the mid-1930s, when Davies replaced them with eighteenth-century portraits, twelve paintings of her, costumed for her most famous film roles, hung in the dining room. There were thirty-seven fireplaces, many dating from the eighteenth century, an art gallery, a "Gold Room" paneled in gold leaf, crystal chandeliers from Tiffany, and a library with a movie screen that rose from the floor.

Each of the fifty-five bedrooms was part of a suite. Marion's was filled with French antiques; it was said at the time that the wallpaper in her room cost seventy-five hundred dollars, several times the average annual U.S. wage in the early 1920s. Hearst's suite was filled with dark oak and mahogany furniture and connected to Davies's by a hidden staircase. Before the couple moved in in 1926, the cost had passed $3.5 million (maybe forty million in today's dollars), of which more than half went into the furnishings. Seventy-five wood carvers worked for a year on the balustrades alone.

To keep all of it running required thirty-two full-time servants.

Worried about living on the coast in wartime, Hearst moved to San Simeon in 1941. In 1945, as part of a program to lower Hearst's expenses in maintaining five mansions in locations that spanned the continent from Sands Point, Long Island, to Oregon, Davies sold Ocean House. The most she was able to get for it was six hundred thousand dollars, the original cost of the fireplaces alone.

After serving as a private beach club, it was a hotel for a time before being deeded to the State of California in 1956. Five years earlier Hearst had died at the age of eighty-nine in Marion's Beverly Hills home, in the room where, in 1953, John, the son of Hearst's old friend Joseph Kennedy, and his new bride, Jackie, spent their honeymoon.

In June 1956, most of Marion's beloved Ocean House was demolished by its new owner, ostensibly to make room for a motel. Although she had sold it, she took its destruction hard and suffered a stroke three weeks later. "We blondes seem to be falling apart," she told gossip columnist Hedda Hopper, referring both to herself and to the highly publicized travails of a blonde from the current generation, Marilyn Monroe. Davies died from cancer of the jaw five years later, on September 22, 1961.

For a generation, all that remained of Ocean House was a parking lot, the original seven-thousand-square-foot, seventeen-bedroom north guest wing, and the pool, stripped of its bridge, decaying in the sun and sea air. In 1990, a new building was erected where the main part of Ocean House once stood, which became a facility of the Santa Monica State Beach, rented for weddings and receptions.

Before settling permanently in Santa Monica, Charles Laughton and hi
wife, Elsa Lanchester, would stay at Hollywood's most famous (and infa
mous) hostelry, the Garden of Allah. Everyone who was anyone lived ther
during the 1930s and into the 1940s, including Frank Sinatra, F. Scott
Fitzgerald, Tallulah Bankhead (who once emerged from the pool completel
nude, to be met by the impeccably attired Robert Benchley offering a dr
martini), Ernest Hemingway, and Greta Garbo. Ronald Reagan stayed ther
between marriages to Jane Wyman and Nancy Davis (whose godmother, th
actress Alla Nazimova, built the place), and Humphrey Bogart and Laure
Bacall began their romance. Today the site is a mini-mall.

The Garden of Allah—the Apple in Hollywood's Eden

When Charles Laughton and Elsa Lanchester were photographed at the door to their bungalow at the Garden of Allah in 1933, the legendary hotel was just entering its golden years. Lorded over by actor-humorist Robert Benchley, the place had already become synonymous with glamour. Tourists were beginning to gather in droves outside, hoping to glimpse the arrival or departure of a star or star maker. They were rarely disappointed.

Frank Sinatra lived there in 1941 while he was singing with Glenn Miller at the Ambassador Hotel's Cocoanut Grove nightclub; his apartment was only a few feet from the bungalow where Artie Shaw, then at the height of his popularity as a bandleader, romanced his (and Sinatra's) future wife, Ava Gardner. Ginger Rogers lived there in a two-bedroom bungalow with her mother after arriving in the film capital in 1932 (she recalled once that the cramped quarters "gave us the needed feeling of home"). Humphrey Bogart and Lau-

ren Bacall began their romance there (they lived in adjoining bungalows while making *To Have and Have Not* in 1944), and Ronald Reagan, who lived there for a while after his divorce from Jane Wyman,
could often be found holding forth on his then-liberal politics in the
hotel's tiny bar. William Faulkner couldn't afford the rent; but for nine
months in the late 1930s, his contemporary, F. Scott Fitzgerald, lived in
an upstairs apartment, trying for the third time in his career to find
screenwriting success in Hollywood. It never came; he would die, his
ambition unrealized, on December 17, 1940, in the nearby home of his
lover, gossip columnist Sheilah Graham.

The Laughtons, as is now known, had one of Hollywood's most unconventional marriages—she was aggressively acerbic; he was gay, but
few knew it. The actor, whose memorable characterizations ranged
from snarling menace (*Mutiny on the Bounty*) to the charmingly win-
some (Jean Renoir's *This Land Is Mine*) and who triumphed in his single directing credit, the allegorical masterpiece *Night of the Hunter*
(1955), lived his life in terror that people might find out.

But everybody knew the Garden of Allah was Hollywood's and thus
America's most unconventional hotel, actually *notorious* would be a
more descriptive word. From sunset until dawn it was party time for
the actors, film writers, and musicians who lived there permanently, in
between marriages or homes, or just during a film gig, an oasis of often
childish escape from the paralyzing pressure inevitably imposed by
success in what was already being called "the industry."

The stories were legion. Tallulah Bankhead once emerged from the
hotel's huge pool completely nude to be met by the always impeccably
dressed Benchley offering a martini. John Barrymore, whose love for alcohol was also legendary, probably held the record for the number of
times one could fall into that pool—or any pool—and not drown. In the
early 1930s, you could look out the window of your bungalow and see
Greta Garbo before she wanted to be alone, often in the company of
John Gilbert, her *Flesh and the Devil* costar and lover, or the Marx Brothers cavorting around the courtyard. All of them lived there at the time.
It was also at the Garden of Allah (in Benchley's bungalow) that Ernest
Hemingway met Gary Cooper, who would later star in the film version
of the author's semiautobiographical novel *For Whom the Bell Tolls*.

It all began in 1918, when silent screen star Alla Nazimova bought a ninety-nine-year lease on an eight-room, Spanish-style house at 8150 Sunset Boulevard, complete with 3.5 acres lushly landscaped with tropical plants and fruit trees. It was located where the trolley line then ended, right across the street from where Schwab's drugstore would be built fourteen years later. Rudolph Valentino was an early guest at Nazimova's mansion; it was there he met Natacha Rambova, whom he would soon disastrously marry over Nazimova's furious objections. Chaplin, the Gish sisters, Western star Tom Mix, and the King and Queen of Hollywood, Mary Pickford and Douglas Fairbanks, were also regular visitors. Many guests—among them Carole Lombard and William Powell, who lived nearby—came to swim in Nazimova's pool. It was one of the first anywhere to be lit underwater and was said to be shaped like the Black Sea of their hostess's native Crimea.

Despite a weekly income of fourteen thousand dollars, Nazimova was always broke. To provide additional income, she built twenty-five stucco bungalows around her mansion and pool (at a cost of $1.5 million, somewhere around fifteen million in today's dollars), and opened the place as the Garden of Alla Hotel in January 1927. Only two years later the Great Depression ended it all; she lost everything except the right to live in an apartment over her garage (or handball court, according to some remembrances; it was probably used for both). Orson Welles's apartment, where he carried on his affair with Lili St. Cyr while making *Journey Into Fear* (1942), was the old garage; Nazimova used to hammer on the floor when his typing went on too late at night.

Except for time spent in New York trying to resurrect her stage career, Nazimova (who earned a historical footnote when she became the godmother of Nancy Davis Reagan) lived at the Garden until she died in the summer of 1945. It's said that she never got over her fury about the new owner's addition of a final *h* to her name, reportedly done to add an exotic allure to the place. In November 1945, Robert Benchley also died. As Sheilah Graham remembers, the Garden was never the same.

Some things remained the same, though, at least for a while. The food in the restaurant (in Nazimova's original house) always was, and remained, terrible; the bungalow's furnishings were always nondescript; service was essentially nonexistent; and the walls were paper thin, allowing everyone to hear *everything* and engendering a host of tales. But no one cared; they were all having too much fun. There was no security guard to check who was in whose bungalow, and the hotel's ubiquitous Ben the Bellboy knew how to keep his mouth shut and eyes averted. Drunkenness and hangovers, both during and after Prohibition, were rampant, as were hijinks and pranks. There was, of course, plenty of the inevitable hope and despair that went with the territory, leading to a few suicides and even a murder or two. It was all too much for Margaret Sullavan, who stayed there before and after her short-lived marriage to director William Wyler; she found the place noisy and frightening.

It was also too good to last. Despite relatively high rents, the place never made any real money under a succession of owners; and by the end of the 1950s, it was run-down and populated mostly by transients and prostitutes. When Nazimova opened the Garden of Alla as a hotel, she threw a gigantic eighteen-hour party. Appropriately, when it closed in late August 1959, it went out with a bang, hosting a party for 350 to which more than a thousand showed up, many costumed as Valentino, Chaplin, Clara Bow, and as the lady who started it all, Alla Nazimova (her 1923 silent film, *Salome,* was screened at the party). Francis X. Bushman, once billed as the handsomest man in the world, his wife, and actress Betty Blythe were the only guests present at both the opening party and the wake. The following day the hotel's furnishings were auctioned off; the highest bid was for Errol Flynn's bed. Just as the Garden of Allah's hedonistic reputation came to symbolize Hollywood, its lifetime as Nazimova's home and a hotel—forty-one years—encompassed the film capital's greatest era.

The memories endure, though dimming. Rechristening it Rainbow's End, Herman Wouk used the hotel as Youngblood Hawke's home in his novel of a successful writer who goes to Hollywood. And although she is far too young to have enjoyed its heyday, when Joni Mitchell sang about "paving paradise and putting up a parking lot" in "Big Yellow Taxi," it was the passing of the Garden of Allah that she mourned. For years after it was razed, tourists could see what it all once looked like, viewing a plastic model of the hotel outside the bank and mini-mall (filled today by fast-food vendors) that were eventually erected on the site. Later, when the homeless adopted the shelter protecting the model, it was moved inside the bank. Now even that is gone, stored "for safekeeping." Only the memories—and the stories—are left.

Oh yes, Charles Laughton. The summer of 1939, when he and Elsa were back in Hollywood and living at the Garden again, was a hot one. After spending a long day shooting *The Hunchback of Notre Dame* in those unair-conditioned days, he'd usually head straight for the pool. There he would happily splash around for hours with his familiar blissful smile on his face and with Quasimodo's hump, still strapped on his back, acting as an improvised float.

Shirley MacLaine referred to it as "the white slave trade." Bette Davis fought it and lost. Protesting it nearly killed Olivia de Havilland. It was the Hollywood contract system, the Faustian compact giving the studios near total control over their actors' professional and personal lives. Louis B. Mayer, head of MGM during the famous studio's golden age, was the most notorious enforcer of the contract system, abusing actors from Greta Garbo to Judy Garland. Here Clark Gable, an MGM star, is assigned to David Selznick (*left background*) by Mayer (*right foreground*) to star in Selznick's *Gone With the Wind*, in a trade that worked out pretty well for the actor.

From Rags to Riches via "the White Slave Trade"—Louis B. Mayer and the Contract System

When actress Shirley MacLaine referred to Hollywood's once-ubiquitous contract system as "the white slave trade," she was hardly the first to do so.

For two generations the studios—among them MGM, Paramount, Columbia, Universal, Republic, Warner Brothers, United Artists, and RKO—ruled Hollywood. One of the ways they maintained their dominance was through discovering, grooming, and then exploiting a group of stars who would draw audiences to theaters then owned or controlled by the studios. To do this effectively meant that they had to own the stars as well as the theaters, and the means to that end was the Hollywood contract. In practice it gave the studios total control over the star's career, and the star nothing—except, of course, the possibility of fame and fortune and a steady income if you behaved yourself. And that's why it worked.

In the hands of some—Adolph Zukor at Paramount, for example—the studio contract was far from peonage. In the hands of a despotic studio boss like Jack Warner at Warner Brothers, the servitude could be grueling and dehumanizing; his studio was nicknamed "the penitentiary."

"Slave trade" is actually not too exaggerated a description of the standard Hollywood contract of the era. It obligated the actor for seven years, though the studio had the option of renewing most contracts every six months. (Why seven years? Because, according to agent and later Universal chief Lew Wasserman, there was a California law that anything longer was deemed slavery.) The standard contract gave the studio the right to decide on every aspect of actors' and actresses' professional lives; what movies they would make, who would direct them, who would costar with them, when and how extensive the obligatory publicity tour would be, if and when they could take a vacation. If no work was available, the studio could, and often did, loan out an actor or actress to another studio. A famous example was Clark Gable, loaned out by MGM to David Selznick to make *Gone With the Wind*. In exchange, Selznick signed away a large block of stock in his company, which eventually gave MGM a controlling interest in it.

Another goodie in the contract was "the morals clause," which in effect allowed the studio to regulate an actor or actress's private as well as professional life. The phrasing varied, but a typical example is that contained in the contract signed by nineteen-year-old Ava Gardner when Mayer added her to the MGM roster in 1941. By signing on the dotted line, she, like many, promised not to "do or commit any act or thing that will degrade her in society, or bring her into public hatred, contempt, scorn, or ridicule, that will tend to shock, insult, or offend the community or ridicule public morals or decency, or prejudice the producer or the motion picture industry in general." This language was a by-product of the scandals of the 1920s, but as many commentators have observed, very few human beings could sign such a clause without crossed fingers.

Oh yes, and if they objected to *anything* (the films they were assigned to make, the shooting schedule, whatever), the studio could suspend them indefinitely without pay until they performed as ordered. And as a real twist of the knife, the suspension time was added to the contract. Greta Garbo was a big problem in this regard for Louis

B. Mayer. During her decade and a half with MGM she was suspended at least six times.

Since there is a serious union presence, one might well ask, how on earth could union members tolerate a contract that essentially gave the employer the right to fire them every six months? Well, as one sociologist wrote, Hollywood is far more a company town then a union town.

Those employees, for one thing, were earning the highest salaries paid in America, perhaps the world. Many of them came from poverty and, suddenly enjoying fame and riches, wanted to hold onto them. Even though there were gaping ethical and legal holes in it, the contract system was also a security blanket, assuring actors of a steady income even during the worst of the Great Depression. It certainly provided more security than today's freelance system, where even the most famous actors live from picture to picture. Actually, the studios' logic wasn't much different from that of the military academies: The contracts were justified because of all the time and money they spent developing the actor's career.

The first person to seriously challenge the system was Bette Davis. After winning the 1935 Oscar for *Dangerous*, she wanted better scripts than Warner Brothers was sending her, and she wanted her sixteen-hundred-dollar weekly salary doubled. When an English producer offered her a two-movie deal, she took it, putting in motion a legal contest that did no one much good and ended more or less in a draw. After a British court concluded that a contract was a contract and that Davis had freely entered into her relationship with the studio, she was left with nothing but a thirty-thousand-dollar legal bill. Because she was—and long remained—one of his top box-office draws, Jack Warner paid most of it.

That was nothing compared with the ongoing ruckus created by another major Warner star of the time, Olivia de Havilland. Unknown when she was cast opposite Errol Flynn in the blockbuster *Captain Blood* (1935), she achieved celebrity status in her second film, *Gone With the Wind,* in which she portrayed Vivian Leigh's "nice" sister-in-law, Melanie. (She got the job through the intervention of Warner's wife, again proving the point that it's not *what* you know in Hollywood, it's *whom* you know.)

Nevertheless, Warner contined sending her second-rate films. One reason was that—like television today—the theaters needed a constant supply of product, regardless of quality. Another reason was that producers, then and now, believed that stars could carry a second-rate film, and after all, money was money. And finally, there were those who felt, as many do today, that Hollywood decision makers couldn't tell the difference between good and bad anyway.

De Havilland began refusing the assignments, eventually garnering six suspensions when she refused to make yet another dog, appropriately named *The Animal Kingdom.* Of course, the time accrued during all these suspensions was added to her original seven-year contract. So she decided to sue, her attorney claiming in part that she "had taken so many suspensions that she could grow old and still be on her original seven-year deal."

It was a big mistake. Warner immediately blacklisted her by notifying the other studios that she was under contract to him and that, although she was suing to break the agreement, his company would insist on its rights until the litigation was ended. She was out of work. In 1944, the court ruled in her favor, but Warner appealed, continuing the blacklisting. Since she was still out of work, she decided to spend her time touring World War II military bases in Alaska and the Pacific. Warner even tried to stop this with an appeal to the head of the Army Air Force, Gen. Hap Arnold, who dismissed Warner's request, knowing that the troops needed de Havilland more than a mere studio head needed revenge.

While in the Fiji Islands, with her weight down to ninety pounds and suffering from viral pneumonia, de Havilland learned she had finally won: The California Supreme Court had ruled in her favor and she was free of her contract. Jack Warner had lost. It was the beginning of the end of the contract system.

Contract problems were rare at MGM, and the reason, as at Warner Brothers, lay in the power of a single man, in this case Louis B. Mayer. Few actors dared to buck him.

During Hollywood's Golden Age—or at least the golden age of the 1930s and '40s—there was no more powerful man than Louis B. Mayer (for years he earned the highest salary of any executive in America) and no more famous studio than MGM. For a generation the company billed itself as having "More Stars Than There Are in Heaven." Even the studio guard was actually named Ken Hollywood.

Despite its fame, MGM's movies were among the dullest and the most trivial of those churned out by the studios in their great years. They completely lacked the brittle sophistication of Paramount's product, the frequent toughness of Warner Brothers's, and the broad range of films made by RKO and Columbia. MGM did do one thing well, however: the movie musical, although most (with the clear exception of *The Wizard of Oz*) are now quite dated. In the era when David Selznick made *A Star Is Born*, MGM made *Strike Up the Band*. And when Nicholas Ray was making his film noir *They Live by Night*, what was MGM releasing? The terminally sentimental *The Yearling*.

Today MGM's famous Culver City studio is Sony Pictures, and Mayer's old studio is just a name on an office complex in a mini-mall in Santa Monica. Mayer's reputation has suffered similarly.

Many knew that he had little taste, was a vulgar bully to those he felt were vulnerable (and there were many), capriciously abused and cajoled actors from John Gilbert to Judy Garland. It was said that, ironically, he had little love of the movies, was just a junk dealer peddling different wares, and that his arbitrariness was sometimes nothing more than an effort to prove his own power. Most of the actors who were his property loathed him for his vindictiveness and outright sadism.

Yet he had his admirers, sycophantic or not. Clarence Brown, who directed movies for Mayer for more than thirty years, including Garbo's *Anna Christie*, *The Yearling*, and Elizabeth Taylor's debut film, *National Velvet*, called him "the greatest brains in the picture business." Josef von Sternberg equivocated, with a wonderful simile that skewered Mayer and his frequently staged sentimentality like a pin through a butterfly: "He was, outwardly at least," said the director, "a charming, simple, and sincere person, who could use his eyes, brimming over with tears, to convince an elephant that it was a kangaroo." But it was silent screen director Marshall Neilan who coined the contemptuous description that outlasted Mayer's tenure at MGM and, indeed, his life: "An empty taxicab drove up and Louis B. Mayer got out."

Born in Minsk, Russia, in 1885 and immigrating with his family to

Nova Scotia while still a young child, Louis B. Mayer (B. originally for "Bert," later "Burrill," both invented) started his career helping his father in his junk business. After marrying and moving to Boston in 1904, where he dealt in waste cotton fabric (not exactly rags, but close enough for many detractors in later years), he soon set up his own junk business. Fascinated by the infant film industry, he renovated an old vaudeville theater in Haverhill, Massachusetts, into a successful movie house, followed by more.

Eventually, while retaining his theater chain, Mayer moved to New York, then the center of film production in the country. There he met a fellow Mason, D. W. Griffith; and when Griffith made his Civil War saga, *The Birth of a Nation,* in 1914, Mayer decided that it offered a tremendous opportunity for his new film-distribution business. Scraping up every cent he could (even pawning his wife's jewelry), Mayer bought the exclusive distribution rights to the film for New England. From an investment of a few thousand dollars, he made five hundred thousand (the equivalent of possibly ten or twenty times that in today's money). He may have even made more. Rumors persist that because of the primitive accounting practices of the day, thousands of dollars in receipts went unreported and directly into his pockets. Yet when Griffith was out of work in the 1930s and '40s, Mayer, who could do anything he wanted with impunity, never lifted a finger to help the man whose talent had made him a millionaire.

Film exhibition led inevitably to film production, and Mayer began with a New York company called Alco (eventually Metro). In one of his first films, the fledgling producer gave an early break to a thirty-two-year-old actress who would later become one of the most powerful Hollywood gossip columnists. Her name was Hedda Hopper. In 1917, he opened his own studio (Mayer) in Brooklyn, moved to California the following year, and bought the financially hard-pressed Selig studio in Glendale (which years earlier had made the first feature film shot in California, *The Heart of a Race Tout*).

One of Mayer's first contract players was Mildred Harris, then Charlie Chaplin's wife. Chaplin, always mercurial and obsessive, became insanely jealous, imagining that Mayer and Harris were having an affair. In fact, during a dinner at the Alexandria Hotel in downtown

Los Angeles, the actor challenged Mayer to a fight in the lobby. Dancing around Mayer like a character in one of his own films, Chaplin tripped on a painter's scaffold and fell flat, knocking himself out.

In 1923, Mayer hired the brilliantly talented young producer Irving Thalberg away from Universal and, the following year, merged with his original Metro company and the Goldwyn organization to form Metro-Goldwyn-Mayer. Mayer was the West Coast director and Thalberg was head of production. Mayer was on his way to becoming the supreme force in Hollywood movie production.

There is no question that filmmaking—or rather, running a company that made films—took precedence over his family. When Mayer, his wife, Margaret, and his daughters, Edith and Irene (later David Selznick's wife), moved to Hollywood, the producer was already a millionaire. Yet he rented perhaps the cheapest house he could find to house his family, a run-down shingle bungalow totally devoid of creature comforts or charm. Reportedly the women were shocked when they saw their new home, but it would be two years before Mayer moved them into a more commodious home in the upscale Los Feliz district.

It has been said often that although Mayer worshiped the money (and certainly the power) moviemaking and distribution brought him, he didn't like movies. How else to explain the abuse of his real wealth, his actors and actresses? Or his often tasteless, trivial choice of films, at least after Irving Thalberg died in 1936, films green-lighted simply because they could make a quick buck. For the most part Mayer's MGM is remembered less for its product than because it was the sole studio in Hollywood to show a profit in the Depression years.

Louis B. Mayer died in 1957, six years after he was forced out of MGM by his investors and long after he had lost touch with the public taste. Like the contract system he stood for, time had passed him by.

It's 1924, and a syndicate headed by Mack Sennett, the silent era's "King of Comedy," is building a sign to promote a real estate development. Shortened (from the original HOLLYWOODLAND), often neglected as an eyesore, and on one famous occasion the launching pad for a dramatic suicide, it is today the film capital's most famous land-mark—the Hollywood sign.

Hollywood's Billboard—the Hollywood Sign

After the rolling fireworks on the Thames, the spectacular kinetics of the Eiffel Tower light display, and the infectious joy of the two million revelers in Times Square, Hollywood's celebration of the turn of the millennium came as a bit of an anticlimax. Although the gigantic Hollywood sign was lit for the first time in nearly sixty years (despite the vociferous resistance of nearby neighbors), the celebrations of the film capital, known around the world for spectacular special effects, seemed pretty dull.

Certainly it didn't compare to the drama the sign had seen over the generations.

At about the same time the great Florida land boom was first taking place in the early 1920s, real estate took off in Hollywood. Subdivisions began springing up like weeds in the warm Southern California climate. Easily the most famous, or at least the one that had the most lasting impact, was situated on five hundred acres of shrub-covered hills and canyons overlooking the center of the film capital.

Appropriately enough, the development, headed by the famed director Mack Sennett, became celebrated not because of the neighborhood but because of the way it was advertised. To announce its opening in 1924, a huge sign was built, costing one of the development's partners (Harry Chandler, publisher of the *Los Angeles Times*) twenty-one thousand dollars. It was made up of thirteen letters each thirty feet wide and fifty feet tall that spelled out HOLLYWOOD-LAND. Shortened a half century ago to simply HOLLYWOOD, the sign is today the most recognized physical symbol of the film capital throughout the world.

Constructed of three-by-nine-foot sheet metal panels painted white, the letters were attached to frameworks of pipes, scaffolding, and telephone poles dragged by tractors up to the nearly inaccessible site high on the slopes of a mountain (then called either Mount Cahuenga or Mount Lee) towering above the tract. Each letter, plus an eye-catching thirty-five-foot circular dot a hundred feet below the sign (the dot is long gone), were framed in twenty-watt light bulbs. Four thousand of them were required, and replacing them as they burned out was a full-time job.

In contrast to the neighbors who protested the short relighting of the sign for the millennium celebrations, the original neighbors of the sign were proud of it, rightly considering it a local landmark. The sign could be seen for twenty-five miles in those presmog days, and airplane pilots once used it for a navigational fix.

Like the Hollywoodland real estate development itself, the life and career of actress Lillian Millicent Entwistle are also remembered through her association with the sign. In 1929, Entwistle (known as Peg) came to Hollywood determined to break into films. Unlike many thousands who have had the same dream over the years, she had good reason to be confident. Sound had just arrived, and Entwistle, a graduate of the famed Theater Guild in New York and a stage actress with a portfolio of rave notices, seemed a natural at a time when the studios were raiding New York's theatrical talent pool for "real" actors.

Nevertheless, nothing worked out as Entwistle had planned, despite costarring with the irrepressible Billie Burke to more good notices in a play called *The Mad Hopes* and making *Thirteen Women* (a murder mystery starring Myrna Loy) for RKO in 1932.

Bitter and dejected after weeks spent looking for work, she decided to make her exit from the film capital in a dramatic way. On September 18, 1932, she climbed up to the sign, which she had ridden past on horseback almost daily during her stay in Hollywood, left her coat and purse on the ground, and via a workman's ladder left at the scene climbed to the top of the *H*. From that perch, where she could see many of the film capital's studios, Entwistle jumped, as she surely presumed, to her death.

But like her career, even her suicide was not a success, at least not immediately. Instead of hitting the stony ground more than five stories below and dying instantly, Entwistle landed on a cactus. Despite a number of operations, she died a painful death several days later.

A suicide note was found in her purse, which read in part: "I'm afraid I'm a coward. I'm sorry for everything." What Entwistle didn't know at the time of her death was that the Beverly Hills Community Players had written a letter offering her a role in their next play. It wasn't much (with almost incredible irony, the role was that of a woman who commits suicide), but it could have been a lifeline.

In 1939, fifteen years after the sign was erected, the developer discontinued maintenance (the real estate development had not been successful), and it seemed that the HOLLYWOODLAND sign itself would perish. Soon every one of the thousands of light bulbs was broken or stolen; and by 1945, when the development company donated the sign and several hundred adjoining acres to Hollywood's Recreation and Parks Department, large holes had appeared in the letters where the metal panels had been stolen or blown off. In 1949, the entire *H* blew down.

Then, after the Parks Department decided to tear down the sign because it had become a highly visible eyesore, the Hollywood Chamber of Commerce stepped in and offered to remove the last four letters of the sign and repair the rest. The letters that remained, of course, spelled out to the world, as they have ever since, the name of the film capital itself.

But troubled times had not ended for the Hollywood sign. By 1964, it began showing its age again and continued to deteriorate until the Hollywood Kiwanis Club adopted it and raised forty-five hundred dollars for its restoration. Despite a continuing clamor to get rid of it from many, who dismissed those who wanted to save the sign as hopeless sentimentalists, in 1973 the sentimentalists won when the Los Angeles Cultural Heritage Board stepped in and declared the Hollywood sign a Historic Cultural Monument.

Maintenance would remain a problem for years. Deterioration continued; by 1977, an engineering survey (again) concluded that it was probably best to get rid of the sign. Worse would come. After the Hollywood Chamber of Commerce used the last of the money in its sign fund to replace the top of the D (which had fallen off), the first O fell apart, the third one broke loose from its mounting and fell down the mountain, and that November the second L was severely damaged in a fire set by an arsonist.

Deterioration caused by the flight of the film industry from studios to independent production and population flight to the west side of Los Angeles had pretty much destroyed Hollywood too, by then more or less overtaken by transients, drug dealers, and users. Many storefronts that used to house bookstores frequented by the likes of F. Scott Fitzgerald and Greta Garbo were peddling T-shirts, fast food, and cheap souvenirs to the tourists who still visited the once fabled community. To reverse—or at least stop—the decay, a number of Hollywood loyalists had the happy idea of using the Hollywood sign, for a generation the symbol of the industry's greatness, as a rallying symbol for renewal. As Mike Sims, then president of the Hollywood Chamber of Commerce, said that year, "If you can't save the sign, then you can't save Hollywood."

Rebirth didn't come about overnight, either for the sign or for Hollywood. For a year nothing much happened other than the failure of a Save the Sign Committee plan to raise the $250,000 needed to replace the sign with a new one through a Hollywood Bowl benefit concert starring the rock group Fleetwood Mac. Neighbors blocked the concert, claiming it would be too loud.

Finally, in the spring of 1978, a major advertising agency donated an expensive radio and television campaign, and another group began selling "I Helped Hollywood" T-shirts. *Playboy* publisher Hugh Hefner, then a recent arrival in Los Angeles and one who considered the Hollywood sign "Hollywood's Eiffel Tower," sponsored a $150-a-person benefit at the *Playboy* mansion, which netted forty-five thousand dollars. The *Y* in the sign was restored and dedicated in his name.

Soon after the Hefner benefit, rocker Alice Cooper gave twenty-seven thousand dollars, the price for restoring another letter. He chose the last *O* in memory of Groucho Marx who had died the year before. Then it became a tide. Former cowboy star and California Angels owner Gene Autry (who also owned KTLA, Los Angeles's first commercial television station), sponsored the second *L*. As Autry said, ". . . the sign has become . . . a trademark, like Pepsi or Coca-Cola, to Hollywood. It reminds us of the glamour days, the golden era of Hollywood." Warner Brothers Records soon sponsored the second *O*, and a Hollywood graphics company paid for the *D*.

Finally, it was done. On November 11, 1978, the sign, lit by floodlights instead of the original four thousand twenty-watters, was unveiled to the public. Three days later all America saw the restored sign when Hollywood celebrated its nationally televised seventy-fifth birthday.

From the beginning Hollywood has had a reputation for
welcoming unorthodox religions and cults. The most famous, at least in the early years of Hollywood, was the International Church of the Foursquare Gospel, founded by
the charismatic, flamboyant, scandal-plagued evangelist
Aimee Semple McPherson. Stars came in droves to the
Sunday services during which she would star in tableaux vi-
vants such as that of an avenging angel casting out Satan
with a pitchfork. Here, in the 1930s, she's joined by the lib-
eral Pulitzer Prize–winning writer Sinclair Lewis (*right*) and
the character actor Walter Huston, father of writer-director
John Huston.

God and Mammon in the Modern Babylon— Hollywood and Religion

Hollywood and religion have been partners in a sort of marriage—sometimes a very unhappy and contentious marriage—from the very beginning. Founded to be a model Christian community, the tiny village had churches long before the filmmakers arrived and was also dry in it's early years. The area's association with religion actually began long before Hollywood was officially incorporated as a city in 1903. On January 13, 1847, Mexican general Andres Pico surrendered California to Lt. John Charles Frémont of the U.S. Army at the long-gone Cahuenga Chapel, a branch of the San Fernando Mission, located on the far side of Cahuenga Pass through the Santa Monica Mountains, about six miles from Hollywood.

Although the community later gained and still has a reputation for hosting offbeat religions, it was the mainline religions that first staked their claims. The German Methodist Church built in 1876 near the place where the Hollywood Freeway dives under Santa Monica

Boulevard today was the earliest arrival; the second, the Hollywood Christian Church, in 1888. In 1890, the somewhat peripatetic Methodist Episcopal Church South was built at the corner of Fairfax and Santa Monica, soon moved to land donated by Mrs. Wilcox at Cahuenga and Selma, and, in 1904, ended up at the southeast corner of Hollywood and Vine. Catholics had to wait until 1903, when Blessed Sacrament Church was built not far from its present location on Sunset.

Then a few things happened over a generation that would change the religious climate in the film capital dramatically. First, the movies arrived, bringing prosperity to Los Angeles at large and unimaginable wealth to a few, many of them Jews, who dominated the business side of movies (Gentiles would control the creative side).

At the same time, Southern California was discovered by the rest of America thanks largely to the evangelism of the railroads portraying it as a land of endless summer bounty. The image would bring thousands of retirees forced to live on fixed incomes but seeking the sun; they, especially, yearned for companionship in their new surroundings.

Then, in the 1930s, came the Great Depression. No one knows for certain how many people loaded their lives onto broken-down Model T trucks and cars and chugged out of the dust bowl, heading west toward California's glittering promise. The impact of all these new arrivals, for the most part rootless, poor, white Protestants, was tremendous, however; and many new churches, cults, and sects, as well as hitherto unfamiliar traditional religions like Buddhism, became popular. Author Christopher Isherwood joined Hollywood's Vedanta Temple, still very much alive today.

Populist in welcome, often simplistic in worship, frequently fire and brimstone in theology, the new sects—along with some traditional churches suddenly seized with charismatic fervor—attracted large followings. Unfortunately, bigotry was often part of the Sunday morning message, and the film industry was often the target.

Bob Shuler was a Bible Belt preacher from Comer's Rock, Virginia, who arrived in 1920 after a stint as a rural preacher in Texas and became the pastor of the failing Trinity Methodist Church in downtown Los Angeles. Thanks to his spellbinding, adversarial oratory, which blamed everyone but his poor congregation for their problems (his nickname was "Fighting Bob"), Shuler increased the church membership to some three thousand and added a radio ministry of many thousands more within a decade. He, like many at the time, was anti-Catholic, hated Hollywood, the movies, the Jews, and the theory of evolution. He also prided himself on his populist roots, living on twenty acres of land in El Monte, raising most of his own food and hogs.

In March 1922, his message perfectly coordinated with the hoopla over the Arbuckle trial, he went after Hollywood: "There are poisons here," he shouted, "that shall destroy the home, besmirch the virtue of womanhood, and sully every principle of social intercourse unless a mighty cleansing be wrought!" Not surprisingly, he was a strong supporter of the Ku Klux Klan, which he believed was a necessary effort of white Protestant men to preserve their heritage. He was not, according to his son Robert, prejudiced *per se,* and had once actually saved a black man from being lynched in Paris, Texas.

In 1926, a member of his congregation gave him his own radio station as a Christmas present, setting him on the road to becoming America's first broadcast evangelist. Soon he nearly went too far, accusing Los Angeles mayor Charles Cryer of being on the take, the police chief of spying on him, city officials of permitting pornography in movie houses, and its WASP oligarchy, personified by William Randolph Hearst and the *Los Angeles Times*'s Harry Chandler, of conspiring to silence him.

In 1929, Shuler served fifteen days in jail for claiming on his radio station that theater owner Alexander Pantages and his wife, both of whom were about to go on trial (he for the rape of a showgirl named Eunice Pringle in a mop closet in his theater; she for drunk driving and manslaughter), would bribe their juries. That year, however, a congregant and former Klan member named John Porter became mayor, and for a time Shuler was untouchable. In 1932, he ran for the U.S. Senate on the Prohibition ticket, coming in second to Woodrow Wilson's son-in-law William McAdoo. (After losing an earlier political race, Shuler put a curse on the entire state and took credit for several subsequent earthquakes.) But he'd offended too many people. The FCC took the radio station away from him, calling him a public nuisance (after Hearst reportedly spent a million dollars to destroy him). His publication, *Bob*

Shuler's Magazine, folded in 1933. And after thousands of new war industry jobs arrived in Los Angeles in the early 1940s, the base of his ministry—the economically deprived—declined.

Shuler, died in 1965, leaving a far gentler dynasty. In 1954, his son, Robert Jr., succeeded him as pastor of Trinity Methodist, and today his grandson, Robert III, is pastor of the Riverside (California) First Methodist Church. Because of urban flight, Trinity Methodist was absorbed into Wilshire Methodist Church in 1973, and twenty years later the building, at Tenth and Flower, was bulldozed to make a parking lot the day before it was to be designated a National Historic Site. Ironically, Los Angeles, praised by Shuler for being "the only Anglo-Saxon city of a million people left in America" and "the only such city not dominated by foreigners . . . in which the white, American Christian idealism still predominates," is now the most ethnically mixed metropolis on earth.

At the same time Shuler was rousing the rabble with his rabid parochialism, another evangelist rose up with a kinder message presented with the flamboyant escapism of a Hollywood musical; in fact, the regular appearance of film stars at her services was one of her drawing cards. She was so colorful that a number of Hollywood superstars, among them Shirley MacLaine and Angela Lansbury, have wanted to play her in a movie or musical based on her life; unfortunately, the caretakers of her legacy have refused all offers.

Her name was Aimee Semple McPherson, and the Pentecostal Church she founded, the International Church of the Foursquare Gospel, is still very much with us today. Like Shuler she was a Methodist, but Shuler hated her ministry with a passion, and there the comparison ends.

"Sister Aimee," as her thousands of followers would call her, was born Aimee Kennedy in 1890 and raised on a farm in Ontario, Canada, where she developed a love of the positive and inclusive theology practiced by her grandfather, a Salvation Army captain. After a crisis of faith, she was reconverted to Christianity ("born again" in today's vernacular) by Robert Semple, a Pentecostal evangelist, whom she joined in preaching revivals and married in 1908. Two years later, while awaiting their papers to enter China as missionaries, he died in Hong Kong, and Aimee, now with an infant daughter, returned to New York to work for the Salvation Army. After marrying a second time in 1912, this time a grocery salesman named Harold McPherson, she gave birth to a son and tried to settle down as a housewife, but to no avail. She was, and would ever be, an evangelist.

After divorcing McPherson in 1918, she, her children, and her mother, Minnie, with little more than a hundred dollars and a tambourine to their names, drove to Los Angeles. It was a trip Aimee later referred to as biblical, a spiritual quest culminating in a revelation. When the group arrived in Los Angeles at sunset, she wrote: ". . . the sun, after leading us ever Westward, laid itself like a scarlet sacrifice on an altar of cradled clouds." To Aimee Semple McPherson, the City of Angels was "the antechamber of heaven." And for a while it would seem to be.

She promulgated her message with a vengeance, promoting revival meetings by throwing tracts from an open airplane as she flew over neighborhoods populated by recent arrivals. Before long she was packing overflow crowds into Philharmonic Auditorium, the largest space in the city. By 1923, she had her own Angelus Temple, seating fifty-three hundred and costing $1.5 million. There she continued to captivate the curious and the faithful by staging tableaux vivants in which she would portray characters ranging from a USC football player making a touchdown for Jesus, to a policeman entering the church on a motorcycle to place sin under arrest.

Besides acting, she had a talent for organizing. She added some 250 affiliated churches, a rescue mission, a publications division, several choirs, an orchestra (in which Anthony Quinn played the saxophone), and a radio station, creating an early example of today's "menu" church. She also composed more than 180 hymns and a few musical pageants, all upbeat and redemptive. True to her Salvation Army background, she adopted uniforms for herself and her female bodyguards.

Needless to say, she also had a talent for raising money, which, besides the church, supported her mansion near MGM in Culver City, fine clothes, and a snazzy car. "Sister has a headache tonight," she would encourage churchgoers at collection time. "Just quiet money please."

But hers was also a healing ministry that, as California historian Kevin Starr says, helped "the inconspicuous, the rural nobodies from the eccentric borderlands of evangelical American Protestantism . . . become somebodies in America. Part of the redemption Los Angeles offered was the chance to become middle class—the glory road led to a bungalow." Soon her popularity would rival that later accorded a star like Frank Sinatra; to thousands, she was "God's Little Child."

As the money rolled in, so did the stories of miraculous cures. A "miracle room" in the Angelus Temple was crowded with discarded wheelchairs, crutches, and the leg braces of a ten-year-old polio victim who was so confident of a cure that he took a pair of shoes along when he was brought to her to be blessed. And indeed, he walked away from the temple.

Then in 1926, her glory days abruptly ended. As with Fatty Arbuckle four years earlier, it was a scandal, galvanizing America's tabloid journalists and titillating their readers for weeks, that did her in. It was also a bit of a farce.

On the afternoon of May 18, 1926, the twenty-six-year-old McPherson was spotted swimming off Ocean Park beach near Santa Monica—and then she disappeared. She was presumed to have drowned, but a massive search, in which a professional diver and a church member themselves drowned, failed to turn up a body or any evidence. Then on June 23, three days after an all-day memorial service at the Angelus Temple attended by thousands of weeping, hysterical mourners, she turned up in the Mexican town of Agua Prieta, claiming that she had been kidnapped and held in a shack in the Sonoran Desert. On her return to Los Angeles, a carpet of roses was spread where she was to disembark from the train, and a hundred thousand followers cheered as she drove through the city in a rose-covered car.

It was soon established, however, despite McPherson's angry denials, that she had actually spent the month in a cottage in Carmel, California, with Kenneth Ormiston, a married engineer on the staff of her radio station (KFSG, for Kall FourSquare Gospel). For nearly half a year, LA district attorney Asa Keyes gathered evidence (which included a Carmel grocery list in her handwriting), planning to charge her with conspiracy to produce false testimony.

Not surprisingly, "Fighting Bob" Shuler waded in with a vicious, tract denouncing McPherson, her ministry, and her theology. As he and McPherson alternated their broadcasts on the same radio wave-length, he had no problem reaching her followers. Somehow he found Harold McPherson and had him on the air for four straight broadcasts denouncing Sister Aimee and washing all their old dirty linen. For her part Sister Aimee claimed the scandal was all the work of the devil.

Then she got a break directly due to her fame. At the last possible moment, the district attorney dropped the charges, fearing his case too weak to convict a person of her immense popularity. The evening Keyes announced his decision, the cheering faithful mobbed McPherson and the media headlined the news. But the damage was done. For much of America she had become a salacious joke.

Aimee Semple McPherson carried on for nearly two more decades, preaching and defending herself against the old scandal. She had a nervous breakdown in 1930; Seconal was prescribed. On September 27, 1944, she died in San Francisco of an apparently accidental over-dose of the drug, or so it was ruled by investigators. Many at the time attributed the accident to the combination of a broken heart and the fatigue of endlessly fighting to restore her image, fame, and influence. At her funeral, held in the Angelus Temple, forty thousand mourners passed by the open bronze casket in which she lay, dressed in her fa-miliar white gown and blue cape and holding her Bible bound in white leather.

There the tale would end but for two things.

The church McPherson founded flourishes. It was led by her son, Rolf, from the time of her death until the early 1980s and claims nearly three million members internationally today. They celebrate February 9, Sister Aimee's birthday, as Founder's Day.

And there is a story that simply won't go away, although the church itself ignores it.

When McPherson was buried, in a gigantic tomb guarded by two kneeling marble angels and a heavy iron chain at Forest Lawn Cemetery in Glendale, it was said that a telephone with a direct line to the Angelus Temple was buried with her, so that when she returned (as her flock was certain she would), she could telephone for her followers to dig her up.

If the story isn't true, it should be.

During the 1930s and '40s, the gossip that Hedda Hopper and Louella Parsons (shown here clowning with comics Bud Abbott [*left*] and Lou Costello) dredged up and dispensed to their vast, newspaper readership made them more powerful than any studio boss or celebrity. Vain and despotic, they could make or break a film, use or abuse stars at will, and generally terrorize the entire industry. They often did.

The Second Oldest Profession— Hollywood and Gossip

From 1935 until 1960, one of the most famous melodramas ever written, *The Drunkard,* was performed in a building at 600 North Vermont Boulevard in Hollywood known as the Theater Mart. It became the longest-running play in Los Angeles history, a record it still apparently holds. Even though the building was converted into the Los Angeles Press Club after *The Drunkard* closed (today it is a Korean private club), a theatrically overwrought atmosphere remained, at least among the hundreds of press agents who mingled with the working press at the club. They had all been actors in an ongoing melodrama of their own for years, complete with archetypically histrionic hand-wringing, fury, frustration, and—appropriate to the building's theatrical history—drinking.

The cause of such angst was a pair of vain, fairly uneducated, and despotic women named Louella Parsons and Hedda Hopper. Like many of the other practitioners of the new art of reporting on Hollywood happenings, they went by the name of gossip columnists. And in the 1930s and '40s, the two had more power in the film industry than any celebrity, superstar, or studio boss, a power they used with impunity. Although everyone who counted in the industry professed their love of the pair, the Hollywood establishment from top to bottom lived in constant terror of them and what they might choose to tell their millions of readers. Even their rivals were intimidated. Later, when a colleague accused syndicated columnist Sheilah Graham of disliking Parsons, the lady snapped, "Never! I *love* Louella!"

Hollywood's press agents were especially terrorized. They were, of course, paid to sell a movie or make a star famous or keep dirt out of the press. But if they gave a story (or, more dangerous, an inside scoop about a star) to Parsons, they risked life and limb if they also gave it to Hopper. The gossip columnist thus ignored, however, be it Parsons or Hopper, might well refuse to print any subsequent news from the unfortunate flack, effectively putting him (most were men) out of work. Parsons would carry a grudge for years, so long that she would occasionally forget what the trouble was all about in the first place and start printing client news for the unfortunate publicist . . . if he was still alive or in business. Solving the problem by having the star or the studio head telephone all the major gossip columnists directly was often a way out of the conundrum. But this strategy could easily backfire and, more often than not, ended up making everyone angry.

Someone once called gossip the second oldest profession (the oldest, according to Rudyard Kipling, being prostitution). Who is doing what to whom and how has been a fascination and the daily fare of human beings since we were eating dinosaur steaks for dinner. It's especially attractive when bad news—or dirt—is being tattled, and it's always best when the bad things happen to someone more famous, more powerful, or richer than you are. As the thinking goes, however bad your lot in life, at least the problems/tragedy/scandal/disaster that fate dealt Mr. (or Ms.) Fancy-Pants didn't happen to *you*.

Hollywood made former junk dealers, hookers, and ne'er-do-wells (as well as perfectly ordinary people) famous, rich, and powerful seemingly overnight. It also made gossip an industry. In its heyday, there were more than three hundred journalists covering Hollywood (Parsons pegged the number at 312 in her 1942 best-selling autobiography, *The Gay Illiterate*). And although industry news, still reported in trade newspapers like the *Hollywood Reporter* and *Daily Variety*, was the overt reason for their presence in the film capital, getting the down-and-dirty on what was *really* happening was the real agenda.

Few reporters or columnists ever got the real skinny on anyone before it exploded in the headlines, and just like many employees of today's tabloids, they kept their jobs by making up romantic and scandalous fantasies to titillate their readers. Knowing anything about journalism was unnecessary; in fact it could almost be a liability because most real journalists are sincerely committed to getting their facts right.

At one time two of the most influential members of the press in Hollywood were a former hairdresser named Joe Russell and a one-time physical-education instructor named Wojciechowicz Stanislaus Wotjkiewicz, nicknamed "Bow-Wow." (Since Bow-Wow was married to Sheilah Graham for a time, planting stories with at least one major columnist was fairly convenient.) Neither had any experience in reporting or writing about show business (or anything else for that matter); but since they seemed to know everyone, and it was the era when journalists' success was more often judged by their imagination than their accuracy, no one much cared.

Still the most important stories were reserved for Parsons and Hopper, and woe betide any publicist or star who thought they could go around this media barricade by releasing a hot story to, say, the Associated Press.

Of the two, Louella Parsons, a roly-poly, toothy, former newspaper reporter (nicknamed "Lolly") was the most influential. At one time during the late 1930s, no studio would hire a publicity director without first getting her approval, and many producers consulted her before casting major roles. The reason was simple. In 1922, she had joined William Randolph Hearst's *New York Morning Telegraph* as the newspaper's motion picture editor, but after the press czar read her laudatory interview of his mistress, Marion Davies, he immediately moved her to his flagship *New York American* at the then-unheard-of salary of two hundred dollars a week.

In 1926, Hearst decided to syndicate the Parsons column—now written in Hollywood—throughout his vast media empire of seven hundred newspapers, making her not only the most powerful journalist writing about Hollywood but the very first to toil in what has become a major industry. Before Hearst's move, most newspaper publishers felt that film news would be uninteresting to their readers. The instant popularity of Parsons, whose millions of readers took her every word as gospel, caused most publishers to throw their pages open to other gossip columnists, although none were to reach her circulation figures.

At the height of her power in the late 1930s, Parsons was also heard by millions more on her *Hollywood Hotel* radio show. It was broadcast from the famous hostelry and featured most of Hollywood's top names, who appeared for free; they didn't dare do otherwise, fearing being blacklisted. (She would also blacklist actors for failing to give her a Christmas present and would send her chauffeur to pick them up). Her opening line, "My first exclusive for tonight is . . . ," became both famous and feared. Nevertheless, when *Hollywood Hotel* the film was made in 1937, based on the broadcast and starring Parsons in her only movie role, it was a total flop. Parsons herself believed that the drinking problems being fought at the time by the movie's director, the legendary Busby Berkeley, were to blame.

Parsons was born Louella Oettinger on August 6, 1884, in Freeport, near Dixon, Illinois, not far from the house in Tampico, Illinois, where Ronald Reagan would be born twenty-eight years later. The two ended up as pretty good friends. When Dixon threw a welcome home party for Parsons at the height of her power, Reagan was the top cheerleader of the event, which was emceed by Bob Hope. After a short marriage to John D. Parsons, a local realtor, Louella married the love of her life, Harry Martin, a Los Angeles urologist. "Lolly's Pop" was one of his nicknames; she called him "Dockie," as a diminutive for doctor. Martin died in 1951.

The success of Parsons was due in part to her masterly use of the telephone (she could be called the progenitor of telephone networking), in part to her large, talented staff, which included future columnists Dorothy Manners and Ruth Waterbury, and in part to her accessibility. Eighteen-hour days were the norm, and stars, publicists, and industry leaders knew they were welcome to call her with scoops at any time of the day or night (she was also known to roust major stars out of bed to confirm a story). Even when the fame of her rival, Hedda Hopper, began to grow in the late 1930s, publicists would proudly cite their ability to get a "Parsons break" to attract clients, just as some-what later, publicists' careers could be made by their ability to "break Winchell," New York's powerful gossip columnist.

Although Parsons became famous in the latter part of her career for scooping the sensational, scandalous romance between actress Ingrid Bergman and director Roberto Rossellini while the pair were making the film *Stromboli,* it was in 1933, early in her career, that she scored the coup of her journalistic lifetime. It was a story so big that Parsons actually sat on it for six weeks for fear the news would harm the film industry: the pending divorce of Douglas Fairbanks and Mary Pick-ford. It was the biggest news of its time and in many ways the biggest single story ever to come out of Hollywood, since no single couple be-fore or since has been so universally worshipped by the world's filmgo-ing public. Her second famous journalistic coup was the exclusive scoop in 1943 that the fifty-four-year-old Charlie Chaplin would marry eighteen-year-old Oona O'Neill, daughter of America's greatest play-wright of the era, Eugene O'Neill.

The withering of the studio system, the rise of the independent star producers (who couldn't care less what Parsons thought of their cast-ing), and television eventually ended the power of Louella Parsons. Particularly television. Stars discovered they could be seen by more millions than ever read a gossip column by appearing on early game shows like *What's My Line,* where they could stroke their celebrity, pro-mote an upcoming film, and say what they wanted to say without the risk of a columnist's embarrassing revelations or story "spin." The last Parsons byline appeared on December 1, 1965. She died on December 13, 1972, at the age of ninety-one.

Unlike Parsons, Hedda Hopper began her career as an actress, ap-pearing in a Broadway chorus line before making her first movie in 1916. During the subsequent twenty years, for seven of which she was under contract to Metro-Goldwyn-Mayer, she appeared in more than a hundred films (she was nicknamed "the Queen of the Quickies"). In 1935, after her savings had been wiped out in the stock market crash and as film jobs became harder and harder to get, Hopper worked for a time in Hollywood's Elizabeth Arden salon. Before long she decided to try her hand as a columnist, urged by friends who said she knew more about Hollywood than anyone in the community. She quickly became the hottest property of the giant Chicago Tribune–N.Y. Daily News syndicate and at one point was said to have a daily readership (much disputed) of thirty-five million.

Hedda Hopper was born Elda Furry in a suburb of Altoona, Pennsylvania, on June 2, probably in 1890 (she never told), the daughter of a local butcher. In 1913, while still a chorus girl, she met and married a matinee idol turned theatrical producer named DeWolf Hopper, thirty-two years her senior. Their only child, William Hopper, was an actor as well, becoming famous as Detective Paul Drake in the long-running *Perry Mason* TV series. Elda decided to change her name because her husband constantly referred to her by the name of one or the other of his previous wives: Ella, Ida, Edna, and Neila. A numerologist came up with the name Hedda for her. "It was the best ten dollars I ever spent," she once commented.

Indeed it was, particularly when she decided to remind all and sundry of her name by wearing on her head some of the zaniest hats ever created in an era known for its crazy chapeaus. She was a staunch, even rabid reactionary politically, so outspoken that in the 1940s her syndicate ordered her to stay away from politics and confine her column to Hollywood news. Celebrated feuds with such superstars as Elizabeth Taylor merely promoted her career. Perhaps the best commentary on her career was her own, when she referred to her home as "the house that fear built."

Nevertheless, much of the news that both Hopper and Parsons reported was fairly benign. The house that fear really built was that of a notorious magazine that flourished—if that is the word—in Hollywood for a postwar decade: *Confidential*. During that sad time, *Confidential*, essentially a hard-core evolution of the fan magazines, struck fear into the hearts of everyone in the film capital until charges of publishing obscene and criminally libelous material forced it to change its editorial philosophy in 1957, essentially putting it out of business. Like the tabloids today, few ever admitted paying any attention to the magazines, but as Humphrey Bogart put it, "Everyone reads *Confidential*, but they deny it. They say the cook brought it into the house."

Confidential's rise and fall more or less paralleled Sen. Joseph McCarthy's equally notorious campaign to eradicate Communists in the government. Both destroyed lives and careers. The difference was that, while McCarthy's facts were nearly 100 percent fabricated, many of *Confidential's* revelations turned out to be at least partly true.

Like the tabloids today, *Confidential's* editors paid off everyone in town, from hospital orderlies to hat-check girls to disgruntled press agents who wanted to even a score. Telephones were tapped with impunity. The magazine was not above blackmail either, which is one reason few lawsuits were brought against it until the California attorney general's action in 1957. As Bogart added: "You've got to have guts or your skirts have to be awfully clean before you mess around with those SOBs."

If *Confidential* liked you—in other words, if you played their game by leaking insider news about Hollywood's goings-on to them exclusively—you could do no wrong. Sammy Davis Jr. was one of those who played along; in fact, once after receiving a love letter of a story in the magazine, he actually sent the publisher a pair of solid gold cuff links. And although he denied it, it was pretty well established at the *Confidential* libel trial that producer Mike Todd (soon to be Elizabeth Taylor's third and probably most loved husband) leaked photos and news about himself to the magazine to help publicize his 1956 film, *Around the World in 80 Days*.

Some of the editorial trade-offs were a demonstration of how sordid Hollywood's dealings can be behind the glamorous, glitzy curtain. In the mid-'50s, Universal-International provided *Confidential* with details of their star Rory Calhoun's jail record for robbery in exchange for an agreement to kill a story about the homosexual carryings-on of a far more valuable U-I star, Rock Hudson.

The celebrated gossip columnist Liz Smith once said by way of explaining the allure of gossip: "Gossip is news running ahead of itself in a red satin gown." And that's the attraction. There just might be something there that's too good to miss.

To movie fans around the world, Hollywood's most famous house—at least since the movie was released in 1950—is Norma Desmond's grandiosely morbid *Sunset Boulevard* manse. In few films do reality and illusion collide so breathtakingly as in director Billy Wilder's saga of an aging film star attempting a comeback. The house, which actually existed, was once owned by the late billionaire John Paul Getty. In this extremely rare shot, the film's star, Gloria Swanson, takes a break between shots beside the home's famous swimming pool, constructed for the film.

Hollywood Houses——Reality and Illusion

In the long history of filmmaking, there are few houses that deserve star billing on their own. Even without the unforgettable theme that is easily the highlight of Max Steiner's score for the movie, *Gone With the Wind's* Tara is one. Saving the plantation house is even one of the main plot lines of the 1939 movie. But, of course, Tara was all fake, a product of designer William Cameron Menzies's meticulous resurrection of the Old South. Another house that deserves star billing is *Psycho's* eerie Gothic Victorian; fake again.

If ever a real house deserved star billing, though, most film fans would probably vote for one now long gone: Norma Desmond's Mediterranean-style villa in *Sunset Boulevard* (1950). In many ways its brooding, gloomy omnipresence in the film is as important as the acting talents of Gloria Swanson, William Holden, and Eric von Stroheim.

Sunset Boulevard started out as a romantic comedy by scriptwriter Charles Brackett about a former star who succeeds in making a comeback. Director Billy Wilder had a much darker view of the story, but he didn't know how to realize it until a *Life* magazine journalist suggested parallel stories of an older, reclusive star living in the past who falls in love with a young screenwriter living in the present. Few know that before he offered the role of the tragic shut-in to Gloria Swanson, he offered it to, of all people, Mae West! (She was, of course, outraged at the idea of even being considered for the role of an actress seeking a comeback.) Pola Negri and Mary Pickford were also offered the part and were equally horrified by it. So Norma Desmond was offered to Swanson, and ironically enough, she made it the vehicle for her *own* comeback (a wonderful reminder of the very thin line between fiction and fact in Hollywood). Smart lady.

The script called for Norma Desmond's home to be a huge, grandiose Italian pile, and standing at the corner of Crenshaw and Wilshire Boulevard Wilder discovered this crucial bit of casting. Number 4201 Wilshire Boulevard was a twenty-five-room mansion on two acres of land built in 1924 for $250,000 by William Jenkins, formerly a U.S. consul in Mexico. The next year he returned to Mexico, and the place stood empty for a decade (nicknamed "the Phantom House") until the oilman and future billionaire philanthropist J. Paul Getty bought it in 1936.

It lacked a swimming pool—crucial to the plot of *Sunset Boulevard*—but Mrs. Getty agreed to allow Paramount to build one if when the filming was completed they agreed to fill it in if she didn't like it. (She kept the pool.)

And apparently the entrance wasn't all that could be desired, so the house wasn't the location for the early scene when Holden, presumably at the gateway of Desmond's house, says offscreen, "I had landed myself in the driveway of some big mansion that looked rundown and deserted." That scene was filmed at the entrance to the decidedly not "rundown and deserted" first home of Vincente Minnelli and Judy Garland in the very upscale Los Angeles neighborhood of Brentwood.

There was another problem too. Although the interiors were fine for the story, they weren't spacious enough for Wilder to move his cameras freely, so they were recreated on the Paramount lot. Assigned the task was a design genius named Hans Dreier, who had been brought to the studio by Ernst Lubitsch twenty-six years earlier (the same year the Jenkins house was built). As the studio's art director since 1933, he was responsible for the sophisticated "Paramount look," as it was then called. As Hollywood historian Marc Wanamaker says, Dreier was responsible for the "stunningly pretentious rooms and staircase" in the house and also the "ironic, nostalgic, appalling and touching use of props." The latter included, of course, the pipe organ, the living room furniture (described in the script as looking like "crappy props from the *Mark of Zorro*"), and Swanson's bed, shaped like a Venetian gondola, which replaced the swan bed called for in the script. It was borrowed from Warner Brothers, where it had seen (much) service in 1934 as Dolores del Rio's bed in *Madame du Barry*. The tiles used for the floor of the New Year's Eve ball sequence were exact copies of those in the Jenkins home as well.

Finally, not only are all those framed photographs of Desmond throughout the house actually photographs from Swanson's own past, so is the excerpt from a Norma Desmond silent movie that she screens for Holden. It's actually *Queen Kelly* (1928) and was directed by Eric von Stroheim, who plays Norma Desmond's butler, former husband, and director in *Sunset Boulevard*. Reality? Illusion? Which *is* which?

So what happened to everything? The interior sets were restyled several times for later films, most memorably by Dreier himself for the ballroom where Elizabeth Taylor and Montgomery Clift danced in *A Place in the Sun* (1951). The house was later transferred by Getty to a former wife in a divorce settlement, and after 1953, "the Phantom House" again stood empty. In 1955, its gardens overgrown as in the beginning of *Sunset Boulevard* and its pool filled with trash, the house was the ideal location for the deserted mansion in which Natalie Wood, Sal Mineo, and James Dean take refuge in *Rebel Without a Cause*. Two years later it was demolished to make way for the headquarters of the Getty Oil Company. Today, that building is also gone.

Not long before he died in the flaming crash of his chartered plane, Rick Nelson sold the house high atop Mulholland Drive in which he had lived for several years. Along with its eleven and a half empty acres sweeping down to Hollywood's Franklin Avenue, it brought ten million dollars from a real estate developer. One of the first things the developer did was to demolish the house, and with Nelson's death adding value to the property, he was able to turn a tidy profit on the deal. Among recent arrivals on the site were the recently separated actors Helen Hunt and Hank Azaria, who built a ten-thousand-square-foot home on the property's highest spot.

What made Nelson's house famous—or infamous—is that from the late 1930s, when he built his "Connecticut farmhouse," until his death in 1959, it was the bachelor pad, mirrored bedrooms and all, of Hollywood's bad boy, Errol Flynn.

Flynn was born in 1909 in Tasmania and made his early living as a gold prospector, a hunter of tropical birds for collectors, and a jewel smuggler. Possessed of extraordinary good looks and athletic agility, he was spotted in England by a talent scout for Warner Brothers and quickly brought to Hollywood. When Jack Warner was unsuccessful in attracting the likes of Clark Gable or Ronald Colman to portray the pirate king in *Captain Blood* (1935), he turned to his new contract player, and the role started Flynn on his way to becoming the successor to Douglas Fairbanks as the world's most popular rough-and-tumble swashbuckler. Films like *The Charge of the Light Brigade, The Sea Hawk, The Adventures of Robin Hood* (the story that established Fairbanks's career in 1922), and dozens of similarly genial adventure sagas quickly followed.

Flynn designed his house himself at the height of his fame and dubbed it Mulholland Farm. Although it was originally budgeted at $35,000, costs quickly escalated to $125,000 with the addition of extra wings for a dining room and den, a pool sheathed in black marble, and a circular stable copied from those of Vienna's fabled Lipizzaner horses. Inside, except for some stunning art, including a painting by Paul Gauguin (a reminder of Flynn's South Pacific past), it looked much like any other New England house of its era: lots of chintz, pine paneling, ship models, and "safe" furniture. Until one looked closely, that is. The aquarium, which ran along the walls of the den, was backed with an obscene mural; trick chairs in the bar released erect penises when the cushions were pressed, and the bookshelves were crowded with erotic and pornographic books.

The dining room, the most formal room in the house, boasted a

Sheraton credenza loaded with crystal decanters placed before a wall mirrored to reflect the panoramic view of the San Fernando Valley. Those decanters were rarely full. Unlike Fairbanks, Flynn was a notorious alcoholic as well as a lecher. His wife, actress Lili Damita, never stayed at Mulholland Farm, but Flynn's mirrored master bedroom, where the huge bed was covered with a Russian sable throw and the black silk drapes were embroidered with gold question marks, saw an incredible progression of girls: waitresses, secretaries, jailbait, whatever, it made no difference.

For years Flynn seemed bulletproof. Even when he was accused of statutory rape, it turned out to be a frame-up engineered by city officials who, not getting the kickbacks they wanted from Warner Brothers, decided to show their muscle by sending the studio's top star to prison. (No one ever said the game was played gently in Hollywood.)

Those question marks on the bedroom's drapes, also repeated on Flynn's handkerchiefs, were never explained. There are those, however, who saw them as a veiled reference to his bisexuality, absolutely hidden at the time except to a few partners, including Tyrone Power and, on one memorable occasion, a rising young author in New York City whom Flynn accompanied back to his tiny walk-up apartment—Truman Capote.

And girls, booze, and (sometimes) boys were not the entire story. The other four bedrooms at Mulholland Farm were often filled with pimps and gamblers, and one was later remodeled with an overhead two-way mirror that allowed Flynn and his friends, comfortably ensconced in a new room above the action, to watch the sexual encounters; all inevitably applauded at the point of orgasm. Flynn staged illegal cockfights for his cronies in a special arena near the stables, which housed his favorite black stallion named Onyx and a polo pony name Beaumont. (The fighting cocks were named for various people with whom Flynn was feuding at the time, among them Jack Warner.) There were also kennels with attack dogs (among which were a pair of African lion hounds whose hair stands up like the quills of a porcupine when excited) and a pet fox. His favorite pet, a Schnauzer named Arno, always stayed at his master's side.

Flynn's house was also famous as the site of some of the most outrageous practical jokes ever played in Hollywood. Once, after a paunchy European diplomat had besieged Flynn with requests for an invitation to one of his wild parties, the actor gave in and invited him to a black-tie event. On his arrival the diplomat was met by a dazzling blonde wearing nothing but a tiny apron and high-heeled shoes, who escorted the guest to a "disrobing room" where he was invited to take off his clothes and go out the other door to join the other guests. Stark naked, he opened and walked through the door, only to discover to his horror that all the other guests were fully clothed in the finest evening wear.

But Hollywood's most famous practical joke was played *on* Flynn.

During the last year of his life, John Barrymore, by then nearly totally consumed with alcoholism, made Flynn's house his second home. After "the great profile's" death May 29, 1942, mutual friends, among them the legendary one-eyed director Raoul Walsh, bribed an attendant at the Pierce Brothers' funeral home into letting them "borrow" the corpse for a couple of hours. Supposedly Barrymore's crippled aunt wanted a private final view of her beloved nephew.

They installed the corpse in Barrymore's favorite chair in the living room at Mulholland Farm and hid, waiting for Flynn's return from Barrymore's wake at the Cock and Bull Restaurant near the funeral home. When Flynn walked into the room, he nodded at Barrymore, took a couple of more steps, and froze. He then ran over to Barrymore and touched him; the corpse was, of course, ice cold. "My God," wrote Flynn in his memoirs, *My Wicked, Wicked Ways,* "the light went on and I stared into the face of Barrymore! His eyes were closed, and he looked puffed, white, bloodless. They hadn't embalmed him yet. I let out a delirious scream."

There is another version of the story which, considering the condition of Flynn's memory when he wrote his autobiography, may be more accurate. Paul Henried (who portrayed the resistance leader Victor Laszlo in *Casablanca*) recalled in his 1984 autobiography that it was Peter Lorre who put Barrymore's corpse in the living room of Mulholland Farm. Lorre claimed, according to Henried, that Flynn instantly caught onto the joke, demanded the jokers show themselves, and offered them a drink. And he refused to help them return John Barrymore to the funeral home. There are those who say this is all nonsense, that author Gene Fowler sat with the body all night at Pierce Brothers, and the only visitor was an old prostitute. Nevertheless Henried claims that it happened although he didn't participate.

Flynn spent much of the remaining seventeen years of his life in a haze of alcohol and drugs, seemingly outdissipating even Barrymore. At one point it was so bad that he was unable to pay his back taxes and a lien was placed on Mulholland Farm. He saved the property by making a couple of quick films in Europe but then lost it for good to Damita for back alimony.

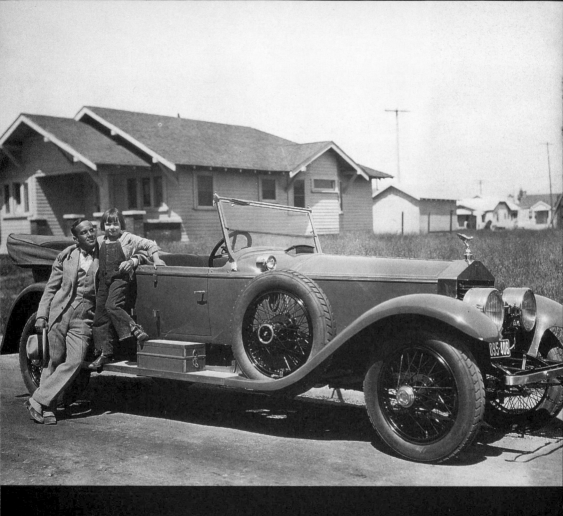

Then, as now, the first thing most newly successful actors
bought was an ostentatious house. The second was an
equally ostentatious car. After the six-year-old Jackie
Coogan made the world weep in Charlie Chaplin's sentimental 1921 film *The Kid*, his family bought him not a car
but a whole Rolls Royce *agency*. Here, three years later,
amid bungalows typical of Hollywood in the jazz age,

Wheels of Fame—Getting Around Town with Pizzazz

Playing the Roman officer Messala in *Ben-Hur* (1926), Frances X. Bushman drove a chariot to movie infamy. The role confirmed him as one of the most famous male stars of the silent film era, right behind Rudolph Valentino (who died that year) and Ramon Novarro, who played Ben Hur (and, of course, won the chariot race).

When he decided to reward himself for his success, Bushman, like countless other Hollywood stars and industry leaders before and since, bought one of the grandest cars he could find. In his case it was a Rolls Royce limousine. And despite the negative sexual connotations prevalent at the time, the macho, married (to actress Beverly Ainge, who drove a black Detroit Electric) superstar had the car painted his favorite color: lavender. He also had the chauffeur, who piloted the huge car down the twisting roads of Bushman's Whitley Heights neighborhood, outfitted in a uniform of a matching hue; even the cigarettes Bushman smoked on his way to and from the studio were lavender-colored.

Ramon Novarro, who was gay (he was murdered in 1968 by a pair of male hustlers), was content to drive himself, becoming a familiar sight in Hollywood in the early thirties as he tooled around town in a dark blue Cadillac roadster. But there was little modest about his car: the car boasted snappy, dual, side-mounted spare tires, a custom interior, and cost about ten times more than the era's basic Ford.

Clara Bow, who reigned as Hollywood's "It girl" in the '20s, drove a Chrysler roadster painted to match her red hair. In case that wasn't enough to turn heads, she had the fur of the twin Chow dogs that always accompanied her dyed the same hue.

Stars loved flaunting their new riches and fame, and the more glamorous or unique the car, the more important the owner. For every modest 1930 Ford Tudor owned by Johnny Weismuller, the most famous Tarzan, there were countless examples of excess such as the huge Mercedes roadster brought by an actress named Lillian Harvey from her home in England when she decided to break into Hollywood (the car stayed; Lillian didn't). Another Mercedes was driven by Richard Barthelmess, the actor made famous by director D. W. Griffith in the early 1920s is another.

Child stars couldn't drive but were also susceptible to the car craze—or at least their parents were. When ten-year-old Jackie Coogan became world famous playing opposite Charlie Chaplin in the four-hankie weeper *The Kid* (1920), a Rolls Royce was also on his shopping list—and not just a car, a whole agency. An early customer was Al Jolson, who bought a 1921 model from the precocious tyke.

During Hollywood's early and golden years, when economic success could quickly eclipse that offered in any other line of endeavor (in the early 1920s the average studio contract player's income was three hundred dollars weekly, half a year's income for the American family of the era and the equivalent of over three thousand dollars in today's money), the dusty streets of Hollywood were filled with some of the most expensive cars in the world. And unlike today's cars—most were nonproduction, custom-built examples of the carmaker's art, many still numbered among the rarest automobiles ever created, the flashiest, most powerful, and occasionally craziest cars ever to roll on pavement.

When you bought a luxury car in those days, especially European cars, it wasn't a homogenized product ready to drive out of the dealership. You bought the guts of the car, the chassis with the motor and running gear, and then either added a factory body or hired a coach builder to design and build a custom body.

There were any number of such coach builders, who could provide everything from a huge, lumbering limousine with a roof tall enough to accommodate your high dress hat to a (relatively) lightweight open roadster. Several specialized in wood bodies, fitted and finished like expensive yachts; one, a French bodybuilder named Weymann, became famous by making fabric bodies (except, of course, for the fenders, hood, and trunk), to save weight. Many, like Italy's Carrozzeria Touring, and France's Gangloff, became legendary for their racy, swoopy designs, copied by a generation of daydreaming schoolboys into their textbooks. Others, like England's Hooper, became known for the conservative majesty of their work. In America, the most famous were Le Baron (who designed extensively for Chrysler), Brunn (who designed more or less exclusively for Lincoln), Fisher (later integrated into General Motors), Darrin, and Dietrich.

Cecil B. DeMille bought a Locomobile, once one of the most expensive cars, to shuttle back and forth on the less than two-mile dirt road between his home and his studio. His second Locomobile was originally built for General Pershing to use in France, but World War I ended before it was shipped. DeMille bought the chassis for the then-astronomical sum of $12,500, had the custom roadster body built in California, and drove it daily for the next decade and a half.

Commenting late in life on Hollywood's automotive passion, DeMille wrote: "The film industry's rise has paralleled the rise of the automobile and, in the same way, the motion picture industry reflects the love of motion and speed, the restless urge toward improvement and expansion, the kinetic energy of a young, vigorous nation.

"It is not surprising, then, that the people who make movies have always been among the most enthusiastic customers for whatever Detroit has to offer."

Before Detroit's models caught on, many Hollywood celebrities bought foreign cars, like the huge Fiats favored by DeMille's friendly rivals D. W. Griffith and Mack Sennett. But by the 1920s, America's motor city was turning out breathtaking wheels for Wall Street's new millionaires and Hollywood's superstars. Gary Cooper's canary yellow and pale green supercharged Deusenberg was one of the most powerful cars in the world, as well as one of the most beautiful in the opinion of many. On the weekends he would often be found in the Mojave Desert with his other supercharged Duesenberg, this one a stripped-down version that he occasionally raced in speed trials. (The Deusenberg, whose astonishing looks, engineering, and performance literally left its rivals in the dust, was the origin of the slang term of praise, "It's a doozie!")

Western star Hopalong Cassidy's 1931 Cadillac V-16 (that's right, 16 cylinders) was one of the quietest cars ever built, and Clark Gable's 1931 V-16 Packard was among the most elegant. Errol Flynn, a notorious womanizer, had a custom-built Packard whose passenger seat became a bed at the touch of a button; its license plate read "R U 18."

In its time—especially the 1920s and '30s—there was no more popular luxury car sold in the United States than the Packard, sold by Earle C. Anthony's famous dealerships near downtown Los Angeles and later at the corner of La Brea and Wilshire.

On any given weekend stars like Robert Taylor, ice-skating legend Sonja Henie, French star Lili Damita (married to Errol Flynn for a time), Dick Powell, Louis B. Mayer, and Irene Dunne (who owned a 1937 convertible coupe with the obligatory rumble seat) could be seen tooling around town in their Packards. Chryslers were popular too, especially the late 1940s top-of-the-line Town and Country station wagon and convertibles (today one of the most valuable classics), which were Bob Hope's and Marie ("the Body") MacDonald's choices in 1947. Lincoln's star-following included Joan Crawford (who owned a late-'20s limousine) and W. C. Fields (who drove a mint green 1935 convertible coupe). Douglas Fairbanks and Mary Pickford had both the top of the line and economy models; among the cars in the garage at Pickfair was a Cadillac limousine and a 1928 Ford Model A coupe.

Cars often starred in movies themselves, from the early chase scenes of Mack Sennett's silent comedies to *The Yellow Rolls Royce* and James Bond's gadget-laden Aston Martins. Remember the Isotta-Fraschini owned by *Sunset Boulevard*'s Norma Desmond? In the

1920s, the Isotta dealership from which the car was originally bought was actually located on Sunset Boulevard. And Erich von Stroheim, who appears to be driving the car in the movie, actually never learned to drive, so the car was moved with cables and human muscle power.

A 1927 Isotta-Fraschini two-seater speedster with an all-aluminum body was ordered by Rudolph Valentino and built on the same chassis as the state limousines for King Victor Emmanuel and Pope Pius XI. Its radiator cap, as on the French Voisin sports car Valentino drove fairly recklessly through the streets of Hollywood, was a coiled golden cobra. Unfortunately, the twenty-five-thousand-dollar car was not finished before the actor's untimely death.

Even when there were only two of them, exotic wheels were a Hollywood passion. Long before Cary Grant and Irene Dunne posed on an Indian-brand motorcycle to publicize their 1940 film *My Favorite Wife,* stars were hopping on bikes. Some, usually the lower profile stars like cowboy actor Buck Jones, found motorcycles an inexpensive way to flaunt their fame, but the big name stars loved them too, from the silent film producer Thomas Ince, who tooled around on an early Harley-Davidson equipped with that de rigeur accessory of the time, the sidecar, to Steve McQueen. Keenan Wynn doted on his Indian bike, complete with leather saddlebags. Even conservative stars like Roy Rogers, whom one would hardly expect to find on a motorcycle, was a fan. Despite his highly publicized love of his horse Trigger (now stuffed and displayed at the Roy Rogers Museum in Victorville, California), the singing cowboy would be seen far more often riding his 1940 Indian "4."

Like many landmarks from Hollywood's Golden Age, most of these legendary cars are gone. Nevertheless, a passion for them still reigns in the film capital, where such stars as Jay Leno have assembled major collections of rare cars and collectors can often be seen tenderly driving an old Packard or Rolls-Royce around town on a sunny Sunday.

First you buy a house. Then you buy a car. Then, before private jets became the ne plus ultra of success in Hollywood, you bought a yacht. Besides showing the impressive scale of William Randolph Hearst's
220-foot steam yacht, *Oneida*, this recently discovered shot of Charles
Chaplin (*left*) and British actor George K. Arthur clowning on board also
sets to rest one of the silent era's nastiest rumors: that Chaplin may have
shot director Thomas Ince (or himself been shot at) during a 1924 cruise
on the yacht. Had that been true, Chaplin would hardly have been a
guest aboard *Oneida* (clearly identified in the background) when
Arthur's wife, Milba Lloyd (a sculptor whom DeMille hired to design the
sphinxes for *The Ten Commandments* in 1923) snapped this in 1926.

Hijinks on the High Seas—
Hollywood's Elite Set Sail

Few actors today own yachts; planes are now the rage. But yachts were the realization of a dream of freedom for actors finally able to afford them in Hollywood's Golden Age. Besides the sense of fulfillment buying a yacht provided a successful actor in the 1930s, owning a yacht was socially de rigeur as well. And for good reason: If you wanted to escape the attention of—and any association with—the hoi polloi, as befit your newly found wealth and fame, what better way to do it than to put several miles of ocean between them and you?

John Barrymore's first yacht was the 93-foot motor-powered *Mariner.* In 1930, the first year of the Great Depression, he replaced it with the 120-foot *Infanta,* which cost $225,000, some fifteen times the average U.S. family income—for whoever was still earning an annual income.

Cecil B. DeMille's yacht was the *Seaward,* as popular an escape for the director as his San Fernando Valley ranch, Paradise. Commandeered by the U.S. Navy during World War II and used for submarine patrol, it was returned to DeMille in 1945 in deplorable condition and subsequently disposed of. United Artists's president Joseph Schenck and wife actress Norma Shearer's *Invader* was an early example of a business tax write-off, often used to entertain film exhibitors on cruises to Catalina.

After Lauren Bacall, Humphrey Bogart probably loved his fifty-five-foot, jib-headed yawl *Santana* more than anything on earth. "Next to being an actor," he once said, "I'd rather be a sailor than anything. A sailor in lots of ways is much better off than an actor. He is safer, he is freer from the restrictions of civilization. . . ." Built in 1935 for an oil company executive, the *Santana* was owned by actors George Brent, Ray Milland, and Dick Powell before Bogart bought her in 1944 to replace his previous yacht, *The Sluggy*. All these much-loved yachts are probably gone now, but the stories of the Hollywood stars' hijinks on them are as fresh as yesterday's tabloid headlines.

In the early 1920s, Thomas Ince was one of the most powerful people in the swiftly growing industry. His mansion, the rambling, Spanish-style Dias Doradas, located on thirty acres near the Harold Lloyd estate in Beverly Hills's Benedict Canyon, was perhaps the grandest in Hollywood, complete with stables, a multicar garage, a pigeon tower, and a trout stream. His Santa Monica studio, called Inceville, was one of the largest of its era. But if Ince is remembered at all today, it's for the scenario that gossip created after his death. If the stories were true, it was more unbelievable than most of the mystery plots cranked out by Hollywood in its century of filmmaking.

On Saturday, November 15, 1924, William Randolph Hearst's 210-foot steam yacht *Oneida* left San Pedro for a weekend cruise, first setting course for San Diego. There, the following morning, Ince came on board. He was then in the final stages of negotiating a production deal with Hearst's International Film Corporation, probably to take charge of Hearst's Cosmopolitan films, for which Marion Davies made all her movies. Joining Hearst in celebrating Ince's forty-third birthday that night were Davies; her two sisters and her niece; actresses Aileen Pringle and Seena Owen; British romantic novelist Elinor Glyn; Hearst's secretary, Joe Willicombe; and Cosmopolitan's studio manager, Daniel Goodman, who was, incidently, a nonpracticing MD. At least that was the official list.

The next morning a water taxi was summoned, and Ince and Good-man went ashore to board a train for Los Angeles. According to a later statement from Goodman, Ince fell ill on the train, and the pair got off in Del Mar, where the director checked into a hotel. Goodman pur-portedly then called a doctor and Ince's wife, Nell, who immediately left their Beverly Hills home in a chauffer-driven limousine with their teenage son to join her husband.

Late on the following day, Tuesday, Ince died. He had a history of ul-cers and angina, and heart failure was the cause of death according to his personal physician. To the surprise of everyone, his body was im-mediately cremated, instantly fueling suspicion and gossip.

Despite the clear fact that he had been on the *Oneida,* the Hearst organization immediately claimed that Ince had been at Hearst's "up-state ranch" (presumably San Simeon), which he was visiting with his wife and two sons. The lie, it was later claimed, was told to spare his family the embarrassment of having it made public that Ince had actu-ally been on the *Oneida* with another woman, an actress named Mar-garet Livingston, who was under contract to Hearst despite a serious heroin addiction.

Then it all exploded. It was revealed that Charlie Chaplin—then at the pinnacle of his tremendous fame—and Hearst's new film colum-nist, Louella Parsons, who was then working in New York City for the publisher's *New York American,* had been on board too. They had been spotted picking up Davies at her studio on their way to San Pedro the morning the yacht sailed. Chaplin was to disembark in San Diego, where he was to supervise a film production meeting. Chaplin's chauf-feur and general factotum, Toraichi Kono, was waiting at the dock in San Diego when Ince (without Chaplin) arrived, and later claimed he had seen him, able to walk but bleeding from a bullet wound to the head. The story moved like lightning through the Asian servant under-ground in Hollywood.

Hearst, it was said, had discovered Davies in flagrante delicto with Ince and shot him. Another even more damaging story was that Hearst had discovered Davies with Ince late at night in the yacht's galley, where Ince was looking for something to soothe his ulcer, and mistak-ing him for Chaplin in the low light, shot him. In yet another story,

Hearst found Chaplin in a bunk with Marion, shot at him, missed, and the bullet went through the thin wooden wall and fatally wounded Ince in the adjoining cabin.

None of this was as far-fetched as it sounded. Davies and Chaplin had indeed been carrying on an affair under the nose of the publishing czar for some time, and he knew it. Yet another scenario had Chaplin bringing along his .38 revolver, which on occasion he had been known to brandish melodramatically, and upset over the prospect of having to marry the pregnant Lita Grey, accidently shooting Ince. (Chaplin married the fifteen-year-old actress, his second wife, ten days later; their 1927 divorce was one of the most lurid in Hollywood history, causing Chaplin's hair to turn white overnight.)

To top it all off, Louella Parsons was said to have witnessed the shooting and blackmailed Hearst into buying her silence by making her the all-powerful columnist for his newspaper syndicate. Although no one confirmed that Parsons was actually on the yacht, no one could confirm that she was—as she later claimed—in New York City either. The fact remains that Parsons spent the following year recovering from a bout of tuberculosis in Palm Springs and became Hearst's (and journalism's) first syndicated Hollywood gossip columnist in 1926.

Many have since denied the stories, but most have only confused the issue.

Hearst reporter Adela Rogers St. Johns claimed in her 1968 memoir, *The Honeycomb,* that Ince did *not* die of poisoning. No one ever suggested that he had. A letter from Nell Ince, published in St. Johns's book, not only says that his death was due to thrombosis but gets the date of his death wrong by an entire week. Chaplin, in his autobiography, claims that he and Davies visited Ince a week after the incident and that the producer died two weeks later. It's difficult to excuse Chaplin for confusing the time frame since he was a pallbearer at the funeral on November 22 and left for Guymas, Mexico, the following day to plan location shots for *The Gold Rush.*

Others have suggested that, in this Prohibition era, it was bad liquor that killed Ince. Considering the grand manner in which Hearst entertained, drinking bad liquor on his yacht, even in this dry period, seems hardly credible.

Even though Hearst knew that Marion Davies was probably having an affair with Chaplin, it is highly unlikely that given his indulgence of her every whim he would have had recourse to killing the actor. Hearst was a very jealous man when it came to his mistress, yet such an act would have destroyed his relationship with the fetching, delightful Davies whom he adored.

Had Chaplin shot Ince, even accidentally, or himself been a target of Hearst's bullet that strange night, he would hardly have been photographed on board the *Oneida* two years after Ince's death, nor would he have been, as he certainly was, a frequent guest later at the couple's celebrated Ocean House and at Hearst's castle, San Simeon.

There is no question that the relationship between the three—Hearst, Chaplin, and Davies—deepened into a close and enduring friendship. Despite the confused memories of the participants, it's almost certain that Ince died exactly the way the unglamorized reports claimed—of a heart attack.

Long before he came to Hollywood, Errol Flynn was a sailor, tacking back and forth from Sydney, Australia, to New Guinea in a beat-up fifty-year-old yawl he bought with three hundred dollars borrowed from his mother and fitted with sails made from canvas left behind by a traveling circus. The boat's name was *Sirocco*.

Years later in 1936, Flynn, still in love with the sea, took his wife, actress Lili Damita, on a belated honeymoon to the Caribbean; it convinced him that one day he would have another ship. Nearly two years would pass, though, before he would get his dream.

In early 1938, with stardom from *Captain Blood* and *The Charge of the Light Brigade* in his pockets, he spotted an ad in *Yachting* magazine for a Boston-built, eighty-foot yawl priced at $17,500. The problem was, as it would be for most of his life, that there was nothing in those fame-filled pockets to buy it—he owed money everywhere. Nevertheless, after cleaning out his trust fund at Warner Brothers and borrowing on his anticipated income for the next year, Flynn managed to swing the deal, renamed the boat *Sirocco*, and hired a crew to sail it from the East Coast to California.

It seemed to take forever, and when the *Sirocco* finally arrived in San Diego flying a quarantine flag, the reason was clear; the crew had slowly wended their way through Panama and up the Mexican coast, and everyone on board had the clap. It was an appropriate christening for a yacht later notorious as the site of a rape charge against Flynn.

There was also a rumor, never convincingly proved, that Flynn was a Nazi spy (the story, with names and scenario changed, was the basis for the 1990 film *The Rocketeer* in which Timothy Dalton, a Flynn look-alike, played a famous Hollywood star who is really a Nazi spy). There was certainly enough cause for suspicion though. In 1939, Flynn made a great show of displaying a collection of small gold ingots that he carried around with him and was seen hanging around with known Nazis. Not only was the private possession of gold then illegal, so was its source. Flynn, in fact, was using the *Sirocco* to run guns, contraband gold, and drugs to and from Mexico from Wilmington, a port adjacent to the Los Angeles harbor at San Pedro. The guns were hidden behind the convertible sofa in Flynn's cabin and smuggled ashore wrapped in rigging canvas.

Flynn was always a sex object, catnip to most women of the time, and they also flocked to the boat—so many that Flynn started calling them the SQQ, for San Quentin Quails. He shared them with his crew (he kept a scoreboard of sexual encounters on the yacht, which invariably proved him the winner), which he dubbed the FFF, Flynn's Flying Fuckers.

All this sexual license got Flynn into serious trouble in 1941 when he was accused by an actress named Peggy Satterlee of raping her twice, once at a party in Bel Air and the next night on the *Sirocco*. Based on the evidence of a consulting physician, there was little doubt that intercourse had taken place; whether it had been consensual was the question. Armed with Jerry Geisler, one of the great Hollywood trial lawyers of the era, Flynn got off, but it was a close call. (One of the most damaging elements of Satterlee's courtroom testimony was her recollection of seeing the moon through the porthole in Flynn's stateroom when, because of the direction in which the yacht was headed, the moon could only have been visible from the other side of the yacht.)

It was a terrible time for Flynn, not only because of the very public trial but because during the trial his current girlfriend, Linda Christian (who would later marry Flynn's sometime lover Tyrone Power), left him. Perhaps more painful, immediately before the alleged rape, Flynn's adored dog, Arno, died while on a cruise to Mexico on the *Sirocco*. It seems Arno had developed a strange habit of snapping at flying fish when aboard the yacht, and at one point during the return voyage he escaped from his onboard kennel, snapped at a fish, and fell overboard. Three days later the body washed ashore near Balboa; Flynn buried the tiny collar in an animal graveyard at Mulholland Farm. Arno was buried at sea, courtesy of members of the U.S. Coast Guard on August 1. That was also the day that Lili Damita walked out of Flynn's life with their son, Sean, and the day before his alleged first rape of Satterlee. After the trial, Flynn never sailed again on the *Sirocco,* finally selling it in the summer of 1945.

His next yacht would be the love of the rest of his life. *Zaca*, a 118-foot sloop, was originally used for scientific expeditions in the 1930s by its first owner, the banker Templeton Crocker. During World War II it was commandeered by the U.S. Navy and used as a listening post for Japanese submarines. When the navy put it on sale after the war, it was in such terrible shape that Flynn got it for twenty thousand dollars (ten thousand less than the asking price). He then spent another eighty-thousand renovating it.

The master stateroom had a bed that was an early example of what would one day be called a California king, extra-long and extra-wide. A mirror faced it, and in the adjoining head was a glass-enclosed tub. Everything was trimmed with high-gloss, hand-rubbed mahogany, and the pine-fitted galley even had an early Deep-freeze unit. *Zaca* had accommodations for twelve crew and twenty guests. It even had its own flag, a chevron picturing a red rooster with the name *Zaca* embroidered below it (another inside joke of Flynn's; try saying cock-*Zaca* quickly).

Since Flynn needed a tax write-off in 1946, he agreed to take the yacht for a cruise with his father, a professor of marine sciences in Ireland, and representatives of La Jolla's Scripps Oceanographic Institute to collect marine specimens off the coast of Mexico. Flynn planned to extend the voyage to include the Galapagos Islands, the Panama Canal, the Caribbean, and finally Europe, altogether a trip of some seven months. After he had assembled what turned out to be a fairly inexperienced crew (plus prints of his favorite films from Warner's library and a cargo of contraband gold, drugs, and cigarettes for delivery to Mexico), the *Zaca* sailed on August 12, 1946.

It was the voyage to hell. Everyone was seasick, Professor Flynn got along with no one, a sailor accidentally shot a harpoon through his own foot, and en route to Acapulco they ran into a severe storm during which the crew mutinied. The engine went out twice, most of the marine samples were lost, and Flynn, on drugs, kicked his pregnant second wife, Nora Eddington, down the gangway. Even when the *Zaca* finally limped into Acapulco, the troubles weren't over: Nora, who had nearly miscarried, flew back to Los Angeles with Flynn's father; the captain of the yacht quit when he discovered the contraband; and the crew disappeared into the bordellos of the resort.

Flynn might have continued on to the Caribbean as planned (with another pickup crew), but he learned that Orson Welles was in Acapulco looking for a yacht to use in his film *The Lady From Shanghai*, starring Welles's wife, Rita Hayworth. Flynn accommodated him (for a then "tremendous price," said to have been five thousand dollars). He also acted as the yacht's captain and technical adviser during the movie's five-week schedule shooting a simulated cruise to the Caribbean (during which Welles first tried cocaine). After filming was completed, Flynn continued his journey.

After the *Zaca* was forced into harbor at Kingston, Jamaica, by a storm, Flynn sold his contraband gold—although he was probably exaggerating, he later confided to a friend that he had $350,000 in gold bullion hidden in the tar lining of *Zaca*'s hold—and continued on to Haiti (where he indulged his fascination for voodoo), Venezuela, and Buenos Aires, where he met and romanced Eva Peron, the wife of Argentina's director. Thus commenced a love affair that lasted until her death five years later. (Once when Flynn was in Buenos Aires visiting Eva, Juan Peron found out and told him that if he hadn't left the country within twenty-four hours he would be found dead in his room.) All this time Flynn was also shooting a documentary called *The Cruise of the "Zaca."*

Back in Hollywood in March 1947, Flynn immediately began plans for another cruise the following year, this one ostensibly to study the mating habits of whales, but it never happened. During the summer of 1948, he and Nora were in Jamaica, where Flynn was planning to build a marine biological laboratory for his father, and living on the *Zaca* (which had been sailed there separately). The project didn't work out, nor was Flynn successful in picking up the continuity and finishing *The Cruise of the "Zaca"* as he had planned. After years of abuse that would have killed a physically lesser man, Flynn's health was cracking. He was also beginning to behave irrationally because of his longtime drug addiction, and it terrified Eddington.

By mid-1950, divorced from Nora and, with drugs no longer calming him down, Errol was in trouble with his studio and losing friends. He met a young singer and dancer named Patrice Wymore who looked much as his mother, Marelle, had when she was young. They were married in Monaco on October 23, 1950 (the municipality declared the day a holiday) and honeymooned on a brief cruise to Spain on the *Zaca*, sailing through a storm so violent that it ripped off the yacht's sail and spars. Later that year Flynn finally finished *The Cruise of the "Zaca,"* which, shorn of the nightmarish images of the trip to Acapulco and the Caribbean, was released by Warner Brothers as a rather pleasant short.

During this time, and with Flynn's consent, a friend named Freddie McEvoy was using the *Zaca* for smuggling in the Caribbean and later in the Mediterranean. There, on one horrible night in October 1951, the crew mutinied, a storm struck, the engine room exploded, and the masts snapped off. Although the yacht finally went aground on a Moroccan beach, many of the crew, including McEvoy and his wife, a French model named Claude Stephanie, were drowned.

Repaired, the *Zaca* was Flynn's home in Port Antonio, Jamaica, during the spring of 1954, where he and Patrice would dine on traditional Jamaican dishes at a table set with the finest silver and china brought from England. They would also barely survive another violent storm during a short cruise.

Flynn had for some time been fascinated with the Batista regime in Cuba and had twice visited him. When Fidel Castro began his revolution in 1959, Flynn switched allegiance so enthusiastically that the FBI mounted an investigation of the actor. He also decided to make a movie about the young girls who accompanied the revolutionary leader out of the Sierra Maestra mountains. Named *Cuban Rebel Girls,* it would star him and his new girlfriend, a fetching fifteen year old named Beverly Aadland. Although Flynn did meet with Castro (Flynn lectured the future leader on Caribbean politics), the trip—a misguided effort to establish a friendship with Castro—accomplished little and was nearly fatal for Beverly. She was staying in the Hotel Nacional when Fulgencio Batista abandoned Havana, and she ended up helping Americans escape the island while the fallen dictator's followers were being shot in front of her.

Errol and Beverly escaped, only to return to Havana a few months later to make the movie. By then Flynn was convinced that Castro was a Communist, and Castro, for his part, had been warned that *Cuban Rebel Girls* would be critical of him. In the resulting contretemps, the only thing Flynn and Aadland could do was again to flee. Lacking the *Zaca* (then in the Mediterranean), they, along with the cast and crew, boarded a rusty freighter, which took them through yet another storm (Flynn seemed to attract them) to Key West. During the trip Beverly took a photograph of Flynn, a sailor all his life, wearing his captain's hat and vomiting violently over the side. The actor was so furious he threw her camera overboard.

Flynn had a heart attack in July 1959, and after several months spent in Jamaica working on proofs of his autobiography, *My Wicked, Wicked Ways,* decided to sell the *Zaca.* A Vancouver businessman offered one hundred fifty thousand dollars, and the couple flew there to finalize the sale. On October 14, with the sale essentially completed, Flynn suffered his fatal heart attack. Selling the yacht was his last act. Edward Bulwer-Lytton *(The Last Days of Pompeii),* who once wrote "Live fast, die young, and leave a good-looking corpse" certainly wasn't thinking about Errol Flynn. When he died he was only fifty years old, but according to the coroner he had the body of a man at least seventy-five.

According to one biographer, Charles Higham, when last heard of the *Zaca* was lying abandoned, forgotten, and rusting away in the south of France.

Christian Speaking
Hollywood Bowl   Aug 2-23
Traveling BEAUSEANT K.T.   5

From its early years, when it attracted such world-famous musicians as pianist Vladimir Horowitz, violinist Jascha Heifetz, and composer Igor Stravinsky, the Hollywood Bowl has been one of the most famous outdoor concert venues in the world. When this photograph was taken in August 1923, keen-eyed concertgoers could spot the urns from the set of that year's big movie, *The Thief of Baghdad*, as well as columns from *Robin Hood* (1921). Along with other portions of the movie sets, they were a gift from the stars of both films, Douglas Fairbanks and his wife, Mary Pickford

The Haven of the Homeless— Hollywood's Intellectual Elite

The Hollywood Bowl is probably the world's most famous outdoor concert venue, its arched shell a visual icon of musical achievement. And in an odd sort of Hollywood way, the world has to thank the King and Queen of silent film, Doug Fairbanks and Mary Pickford, for at least part of its success.

Here's how it happened: Soon after the Bowl opened on August 11, 1922, it was apparent that a fairly permanent stage and concert shell was desperately needed. It would have been impossible, given the shaky finances of the operation, had not Douglas Fairbanks and Mary Pickford donated parts of the sets left over from Fairbanks's 1921 film *Robin Hood*, at the time the biggest production—in dollars *and* size (crucial for the scale of the new stage)—ever seen in Hollywood. At least two props—a pair of huge urns—from Fairbanks's just completed 1923 film, *The Thief of Bagdad*, were donated and used as well.

Despite the stars' generosity, more was needed. The canvas roof, for example, that could be stretched over the stage or removed for spectaculars like the Easter morning service, did little to keep out the elements. In 1927, five years after the Bowl opened, architect Frank Lloyd Wright Jr., son of the century's most famous architect and always known as Lloyd, was commissioned to design its first concert shell. It was quickly built and, following the design lead of Lloyd's father, had a distinctly Mayan look about it.

No one much liked the shell, so the next year, Lloyd was asked to redesign it and came up with one made of concentric half-rings, which was replaced by the present similarly designed steel-reinforced shell for the opening of the 1929 season.

The Hollywood Bowl was funded by Christine Wetherill Stevenson, heiress to a Pittsburgh paint fortune, who had landed in Hollywood in 1918 with the idea of bringing culture to the town by presenting religious plays. With a friend, she bought a piece of hillside land shaped like a natural amphitheater and possessing perfect acoustics. They spent forty-nine thousand dollars for it in September 1919.

Originally known as Daisy Dell, the place got its present name the following year when Hugo Kitchhofer, directing Lionel Barrymore in a theatrical production (with the Hollywood Community Chorus) called *The Landing of the Pilgrims,* exclaimed, "It's like a big bowl, a Hollywood Bowl!" True to Stevenson's original intention of using the spot for religious presentations, the first of the world-famous Easter sunrise services took place there on March 21, 1921. Stevenson finally achieved her original goal soon afterward when she moved her operations across the street to the Pilgrimage Theater.

A year after a warmup concert by the Los Angeles Symphonic Band, things got seriously underway at the Hollywood Bowl on July 11, 1922, when an audience of eight hundred sat down on the long wooden benches erected on the hillside to hear conductor Alfred Hertz and the Los Angeles Philharmonic launch the first season of music under the stars. That season, thirty-six thousand tickets were sold at twenty-five cents each for a gross of nine thousand dollars. Today more than a million tickets are sold each summer, and the cheapest is still only a dollar. There were no facilities for eating (other than picnicking, still popular today), and audience members parked their Tin Lizzies in the sagebrush behind the raised wooden orchestra platform. By 1925, the venue had become so popular that more than four thousand sticks of dynamite were exploded to loosen nearly forty thousand cubic yards of dirt, which were hauled away by mule teams to create today's symmetrical, three-acre seating area.

In the years to come, many of the world's most famous musicians would perform at the Hollywood Bowl. How they all ended up in Hollywood and what they—along with important architects, writers, and educators—did while they were there makes a fascinating story. So important were their contributions to the community's cultural life in the 1930s and into the 1940s that Los Angeles, often disparaged today as "la-la-land," was for a while the world's music capital. It was also at least New York City's equal in literary resources and talent.

It has been estimated that about half of the European (and four-fifths of the German-speaking) intellectual and creative talent moved to this relatively small patch of California's coast during this time. Most of them came to escape Nazi persecution. "It was a mass migration of a thrown-together elite unprecedented in history," says Hollywood Bowl Museum director Dr. Carol Merrill-Mirsky. The migration included filmmakers too, talents like Billy Wilder, who in December 1935, newly arrived from Germany, was living in an anteroom outside the women's toilets in the basement of the Chateau Marmont Hotel. In only a few years he would begin his rise to fame with *The Major and the Minor* (1941), succeeded by such classics as *The Lost Weekend, Sunset Boulevard, The Seven Year Itch,* and *Some Like It Hot.*

Refugees from Vichy France included filmmakers René Clair, Max Ophuls, and Jean Renoir. Renoir was accompanied by *The Little Prince*'s author Antoine de Saint-Exupéry, who needed a peaceful setting in which to finish his novel *Vol de Nuit.*

Among the newly arrived political exiles were several of the greatest musicians and composers of the twentieth century. On a given day it wouldn't have been too hard to assemble a group unmatched anywhere else in the musical world. Hosted perhaps by Anna Werfel (widow of Gustav Mahler, ex-wife of the great Bauhaus architect Walter Gropius, and then married to *Song of Bernadette* author Franz Werfel), the gathering could hypothetically include the composers Igor Stravinsky, Ernest Krenek, Arnold Schoenberg, George Antheil, and Sergei Rachmaninoff. Also invited could be the greatest violinist in the world Jascha Heifetz, the equally eminent pianists Vladimir Horowitz and Arthur Rubinstein, and the legendary conductors Bruno Walter and Otto Klemperer. (Klemperer was music director of the Los Angeles Philharmonic from 1933 to 1939.) Bend the dates a bit more, and Anna Werfel's gathering could include the Russian violinist Nathan Milstein, the German cellist Emmanuel Feuermann, and the Russian cellist Gregor Piatagorsky.

Although the wartime years generated plenty of pop music, it was classical music that drew huge audiences to weekly radio broadcasts by the New York Philharmonic, the NBC Symphony (formed by the network's president, David Sarnoff, for Arturo Toscanini), the Firestone Hour with its major opera stars, and the Longine's Symphonette. And, of course, to the Hollywood Bowl. In fact, although the Beatles debuted there in 1964, and despite performances by such superstars as Frank Sinatra, Judy Garland, Elton John, Billie Holliday, and Nat "King" Cole (even Franklin Delano Roosevelt in a 1936 campaign appearance), the all-time attendance record at the Bowl—26,410—was set on August 7, 1936, by the diminutive French coloratura soprano Lily Pons.

"I came to California for the first time in 1927," said Bruno Walter. "I had to conduct a concert at the Hollywood Bowl, and fell in love with it at first sight," he recalled. "After that I always wanted to make my domicile here, but only in 1935 could I do so." Walter was one of the few arrivals who wasn't running from Hitler; he was fleeing, as he said, from the *"allegro furioso"* of New York City to the *"allegretto grazioso"* of Beverly Hills.

In addition to the musicians, there were the writers. William

Faulkner and F. Scott Fitzgerald worked off and on for the studios for years. The great German writer Thomas Mann lived happily in Pacific Palisades; his less talented brother Heinrich toiled unhappily for $125 a week in the script department at MGM. Franz Werfel was there with his wife and also writing—somewhat more successfully than Heinrich Mann—filmscripts.

Also in Hollywood were the playwright Berthold Brecht; the writer Christopher Isherwood (whose *Berlin Diaries,* a memoir of that city's between-the-wars decadence, was adapted as a movie, *I Am a Camera,* and the musical *Cabaret*); the stage director Max Reinhard; and trailblazing architects like Berlin's Rudolph Schlindler and Vienna's Richard Neutra. The Russian-American sculptor Alexander Archipenko lived there too, as did the famed German philosophers Ludwig and Herbert Marcuse.

Viennese *wunderkind* composer Eric Wolfgang Korngold made the transition to writing music for films very successfully; his scores for *The Adventures of Robin Hood* (1935), which starred Errol Flynn, and *King's Row* (1941), in which Ronald Reagan made a name for himself, are still heard often, even occasionally in pops outings at the Hollywood Bowl.

Less successful was composer Arnold Schoenberg's encounter with the film industry. Schoenberg, inventor of music's controversial twelve-tone system, fled his native Berlin in 1933 and settled in California because of his chronic asthma. Irving Thalberg, the production chief of MGM, heard the composer's romantic *Verklarte Nacht* one afternoon on a New York Philharmonic radio broadcast. Discovering that the composer lived in his own backyard, Thalberg summoned him to discuss composing a score for his current film project, Pearl Buck's *The Good Earth.* The reclusive Schoenberg, earning five thousand dollars a year as a UCLA professor, was tempted when a mutual friend of his and Thalberg's suggested that the fee might be in the neighborhood of twenty-five thousand dollars and agreed to a meeting. It was a disaster. Since *The Good Earth* was a story set in China, Thalberg said he wanted "Oriental music." Schoenberg ignored him, claimed that most movie music was dull and meaningless, demanded complete control of all the sound in the film, not only the music but the dialogue, and added that the actors would have to speak in the same pitch and key as the music he wrote.

It was obvious that composer and producer were not speaking the same language (literally as well as figuratively; everything was translated by their mutual friend Salka Viertel). Nevertheless, Thalberg ushered Schoenberg out of the office and asked him to read and think about the script. The composer did and had his wife call the next day demanding fifty thousand dollars for the job. "I almost agreed to write music for a film," he later wrote to Alma Mahler Gropius Werfel, "but fortunately asked $50,000, which, fortunately, was too much, for it would have been the end of me."

Others were not so lucky. Igor Stravinsky's avant-garde ballet *Le Sacre du Printemps (The Rite of Spring)* was transformed by Walt Disney in *Fantasia* (1939) into "an unresisting imbecility," according to the composer. Nevertheless, Hollywood's checkbook culture overcame his prejudices years later when Stravinsky sold options to the scores of two other ballets, *Renard* and *The Firebird,* to Disney's company.

In 1946, film composer Dimitri Tiomkin was asked by David O. Selznick to write "some orgasm music" for *Duel in the Sun,* a film in which Gregory Peck and Jennifer Jones are notoriously miscast as villains who end up shooting each other. When nothing Tiomkin composed satisfied the producer, Selznick snapped, "I like it, but it isn't orgasm music. It's not *shtump*; it's not the way I fuck!" To which Tiomkin replied, "Mr. Selznick, you fuck your way, I'll fuck my way. To me, *that* is fucking music."

Still, there was the Hollywood Bowl. Sergei Rachmaninoff moved to Beverly Hills in 1942 for his health but died there the following year. Ten months before his death he appeared at the Hollywood Bowl as part of an all-Russian program. In August 1942, he visited the Bowl to hear the great Russian pianist Vladimir Horowitz play his Third Piano Concerto. Before an audience of twenty-three thousand, Rachmaninoff walked onto the stage after the performance to congratulate Horowitz for playing his music "the way I have always dreamed that . . . it should be played, but never expected to hear it that way on earth." Horowitz remembered the moment as "the greatest . . . of my life." It was Sergei Rachmaninoff's last public appearance.

And for thousands of Southern California residents, the time still lives in their memories as among the greatest and most rewarding of their lives.

By 1929, when this photograph was taken, the career of Clara Bow (*center*), the sexy, vivacious "It girl" of the flapper generation, was on its way down. Like many before and since, it was the victim of the actress's mistake in believing her own publicity and trying to continue in real life the fantasy life she played on-screen. Nevertheless, if you're a star, you have to keep up the act regardless of circumstances. In this picture, although Bow could probably have picked an escort more glamorous than Charlie Murray, a Mack Sennett comedian thirty-three years her senior, she was at least in the right place. For more than a generation there was no better place to be seen than the Cocoanut Grove nightclub.

the 1930s, '40s, and '50s as well as for Manhattan's covey of newspaper columnists. In Hollywood the same was true of the Trocadero, Mocambo, and Ciro's, all located on an unincorporated part of Sunset Boulevard called "the Strip."

But the most famous playground for a generation of movie stars was the Cocoanut Grove, located in the Ambassador Hotel on Wilshire Boulevard. Today the empty shell of the Grove (as everyone called it) and the hotel that housed it still stand, decaying, in the center of a dispute over the fate of the fifty-plus-acre property, but the sights, sounds, and celebration that made the Cocoanut Grove one of the most famous nightclubs in the world have long since faded.

It all began in April 1921, when the club's host, Johnny Manos, heard from his friend Valentino that a number of fake palm trees used in the filming of the Latin Lover's hit film *The Sheik* were left over and available for under five hundred dollars. Manos bought and installed them in the space—big as an airplane hangar—at the Ambassador, and a legend was born. Countless actors, including Charlie Chaplin and Pola Negri, would discover romance under those palms. And newly arrived stars from Carole Lombard to Joan Crawford would go there to compete for silver dance trophies (Crawford got into instant hot water with her boss, Louis B. Mayer, by displaying too much flesh in those contests).

From Errol Flynn, Howard Hughes, and Mary Pickford to Gloria Swanson and Marlene Dietrich, everyone who was anyone in the film colony considered the Cocoanut Grove a home away from home, and woe betide anyone who dared sit at their regular tables (thanks to Manos, that rarely happened). Tuesday was the big night at the Grove and the usual evening for special events like Charleston contests or Greenwich Village night (when everyone came dressed as an artist, writer, or poet). It was also the night for special decorations like toy monkeys for men to pluck from the trees for their dates. (There were never enough, which, fueled by bootleg liquor from hip flasks, inevitably led to fisticuffs; by 1937, publicists for the club were proudly asserting that 126 major celebrity fights had taken place there.) Lionel Barrymore solved the toy monkey problem unforgettably one evening

Paper Palms and Chocolate Sodas— Dining and Dancing Through Hollywood's Glamour Days and Nights

Though they often claim to long for privacy, film stars are by definition very public people. Publicity drives the fame, and it has ever since the film industry early on bowed to moviegoers' demands and began identifying the previously anonymous actors. Today the appetite of the public for news and gossip about its favorite stars, especially details about how and where they relax, even where and what they eat, remains insatiable.

Today a star can garner incredible publicity benefits unavailable to an actor in the early years of Hollywood simply by going on the *Tonight Show*; one appearance will reach as many people as probably saw a pre-television-era actor in all the films they may have made. In the era when newspapers ruled, however, a sure way of "getting ink" was by being seen (and occasionally making a fool of oneself) in the great nightclubs of New York and Hollywood. New York's legendary El Morocco and Stork Club were magnets for the paparazzi of when he released a cage of live monkeys, terrifying many inebriated guests.

Singers from Bing Crosby (who was discovered there by Mack Sennett) to Frank Sinatra headlined at the Grove. Even a young Judy Garland, still using her birth name of Frances Gumm, was showcased. The floor shows were also infamous for the tableaux and floats, which carried bevies of near-naked showgirls. There was nothing "near-nude" about the girl that costume designer Adrian placed inside a gigantic ice cube one night; she was completely naked and was kept from freezing by an electric coil inside her hollow iceberg.

When Prohibition was repealed, Billy Wilkerson, the powerful owner of the *Hollywood Reporter,* began storing the wine and spirits he was importing in an abandoned building that had once been a speakeasy on Sunset Strip. (Incidentally, there were far fewer speakeasies in Los Angeles during Prohibition than in New York; stars preferred to have their spirits delivered directly to their doors by bootleggers like Tony Cornero and Frank Orsati, who supplied the needs of Louis B. Mayer.) Eventually Wilkerson hit on the idea of opening the place as a nightclub, borrowed money from everyone he knew to remodel it, named it the Trocadero, and had the guts to claim it was sold out for weeks until it became a "hot" destination.

As at the Grove, hopefuls with talent were showcased; at the Trocadero they included Mary Martin and Martha Raye. But the "discovery" that made the fame of the place was that of Rita Hayworth, and the story that became legend in Hollywood was as spurious as Wilkerson's "sold-out" claims when the place opened. It was at the "Troc," so the story went, that Columbia boss Harry Cohn (or director Howard Hawks) noticed a young actress and dancer named Margarita Cansino, changed her name, and made her famous. Nothing, in fact, could be further from the truth. By the time she played Richard Barthelmess's wife in the first film she did for Hawks, *Only Angels Have Wings,* (1939), Hayworth was the veteran of nearly thirty films, made under both her own name and her screen name. Nevertheless, whether it was in the Trocadero or not, it was Hawks who saw and developed the glamorous side of Hayworth's persona that would quickly make her one of the world's most recognized personalities.

Located near the Trocadero, the Mocambo was long a favorite of many stars, especially Humphrey Bogart and Lauren Bacall (whenever they arrived, the band would strike up "That Old Black Magic"), and it was there that Frank Sinatra first became known in Hollywood.

But whether a given star chose to become a denizen of the Hollywood nights or not, he or she still had to eat. For years, much of America's intellectual elite joked about eating in Los Angeles. Where else could you buy coffee and a doughnut at a stand *shaped* like a doughnut? Or a hot dog from an outdoor vendor plying his trade below a twenty-foot-long plaster-and-lath weenie?

Now many of those camp icons are gone. But even in the silly years, how Hollywood dined—both at work, in the commissaries of the powerful studios, and at play—was glamorized and imitated by millions even while it was being dismissed by the food intelligentsia.

Closest to the whimsey of hot-dog stands that looked like hot dogs was the Brown Derby on Wilshire Boulevard, shaped exactly like the British topper. Opened in 1926 directly across the street from the Ambassador Hotel, the restaurant lured diners in its early days with a sign atop the crown inviting one and all to "Eat in the Hat." Before long the sign was redundant; the place was an instant hit for cofounders Herbert Somborn (once married to Gloria Swanson) and Wilson Mizner, a well-known writer. It was rumored that studio boss Jack Warner was a silent partner.

No one is quite sure how the derby was selected as the restaurant's image. Some say it was because the hat was considered a classy symbol within the newly affluent film colony (surely it would then have been black, never brown). Others say it was Mizner's homage to New York's governor Al Smith, whom he had seen wearing his trademark derby on an earlier visit to Los Angeles.

In any case, the derby motif was pervasive. The light fixtures had derby-shaped domes, the waitresses wore uniforms with skirts starched into a derby shape, and the derby logo appeared on everything from menus to matches to bills. The restaurant also stayed open until 4 A.M., a big draw for Hollywood in its biggest party-time decade.

In 1929, a second Brown Derby—not shaped like a hat—opened near Hollywood and Vine in a building owned by Cecil B. DeMille. Because it was located closer to the studios, the branch was usually packed with stars like Katharine Hepburn, Jean Harlow, William Powell, Charlie Chaplin, W. C. Fields, and John Barrymore; most sat in booths along the north side of the main room below caricatures of themselves. After 1934, when the branch was taken over by Robert H. Cobb, they might lunch, frequently fully costumed for whatever film they were currently making, on the famous and now generic Cobb Salad. If their waistlines weren't a consideration, they might order the Brown Derby's equally popular corned beef hash. Dessert was inevitably the celebrated Grapefruit Cake (which, other than the fruit, is a fairly straightforward white cake iced with cream cheese and grapefruit slices).

The Brown Derbys were the first restaurants where telephones could be delivered to a patron's table. They were also featured in twenty-seven films, including *What Price Hollywood?* (1932) in which Constance Bennett is "discovered" while working at the original Brown Derby.

Today the Derbys (plus two additional ones opened in the late 1930s in Beverly Hills and the Los Feliz area of Los Angeles) are gone, but they live on in a way in Orlando, Florida, where the original Cobb Salad and Grapefruit Cake are still offered at Walt Disney World. The original hat? It survived the demolition of the Brown Derby restaurant in 1979 through the work of architectural preservationists, but just barely. Today painted an ugly reddish orange, it sits above a restaurant on the second floor of a mini-mall erected on the original site. The Derby on Vine served its last slice of Grapefruit Cake in 1985.

One of the most famous eateries of the stars was Romanoff's in Beverly Hills. It was a late arrival to Hollywood—1941—and Jack Warner was a partner along with 20th Century-Fox's Darryl Zanuck. Like the Derby, Romanoff's was an instant hit, and no wonder. The French cuisine was first rate (especially the now-legendary individual chocolate soufflés smothered in whipped cream) and so was the welcome accorded one and all by the restaurant's owner—with his trademark spats, moustache, walking stick, and Oxford accent—Prince Michael Romanoff.

It made little difference that Prince Mike wasn't a prince at all; in fact, everyone who didn't know he was a fake surely became aware of it after *Life* magazine branded him "the most wonderful liar in the United States" in 1945. Romanoff was plain Harry Gerguson, the orphaned son of a Cincinnati tailor. Arriving in Hollywood in 1927, his fake Russian title, slightly twee accent—supposedly acquired when he was a servant working in a British university—and charm immediately ingratiated him with the film colony, many of whom believed that hanging around with the aristocracy—or anyone with a British accent—lent a patina of respectability to their new wealth. In 1931, a member of Hollywood's growing Russian colony guessed the truth, and Gerguson, fearing the consequences, fled the film capital. It would be a decade before he returned and opened the first Romanoff's on Rodeo Drive.

Although celebrities fought to sit at the five booths for dinner, at lunchtime these prime spots were untouchable throughout the 1940s and '40s. The first booth was always occupied by Humphrey Bogart; the second by the founder of the William Morris talent agency, Abe Lastvogel; the third by Louis B. Mayer, head of MGM; the fourth by 20th Century-Fox's chief, Darryl Zanuck; and the fifth by the acerbic head of Columbia Pictures, Harry Cohn.

By 1951, something had to be done about the booth problem, so Romanoff moved to larger quarters down the street, complete with a roof garden, a much larger dining room, and room for twenty-four booths. It didn't help. For some reason the celebrities all wanted to be seated on the left side of the staircase in the new restaurant, where there were only four booths, so the likes of Clark Gable, Elizabeth Taylor, Cary Grant, and even Mae West, loyal Romanoff's patrons all, ended up in "Siberia."

Time, plus the inevitable aging of his clientele and the arrival of new restaurants catering to a younger crowd, eventually eroded Romanoff's patronage. So did the gradual loss of the charm that was his passport to the film capital. When Alfred Hitchcock dozed for a moment after a huge lunch in the mid-1950s, Romanoff made a caustic remark. Unfortunately the director heard him and never set foot in the restaurant again.

Romanoff also offended many film stars, most of whom were Democrats, by not only becoming an ultraconservative Republican and loudly proclaiming his close friendship with FBI chief J. Edgar Hoover, but by placing conservative political tracts on the restaurant's tables.

Romanoff's closed for good on New Years Eve, 1962. The next day, director Billy Wilder hired Romanoff's maître d'hôtel, Kurt Niklas, to be the host of a new restaurant that he, Jack Benny, Otto Preminger, and Jack Warner (again) were opening. It was called The Bistro, and it quickly became the restaurant of choice for an entire new generation of Hollywood superstars and power brokers.

Standing forlornly near the intersection of Wilshire and Western, directly across the street from the restored Los Altos Apartments (where Marion Davies once cavorted in a huge, two-level spread, and Judy Garland once lived), is the sad, peach-colored shell of Perino's Restaurant. In its day there was no more elegant place to dine in Hollywood, and—if recognizability of patrons, elegance of dress, and sheer weight of jewelry are the criteria—possibly in the United States. In the 1930s, fans and the paparazzi kept vigil at Perino's hoping, just as they did at premieres, for glimpses of their favorite stars arriving and leaving under the famous porte cochere. All this despite the intense antipathy of Perino's regular patrons, the WASP denizens of the nearby gated Hancock Park community, to the film industry itself. (Of course, many Hancock Park residents, like Earle C. Anthony, who owned the Packard agency, made very good livings off the film industry.)

The food was good—not great, just good. By some alchemy, Angelo Perino, an immigrant from the Lake Como region of northern Italy who originally wanted to be a blacksmith, evolved an early light spin on the rich Italo-French cuisine of that region. Sanitized, too; he never allowed garlic in any of his dishes.

Angelo Perino came to America at the age of fifteen and worked his way up from busboy to maître d'hôtel in the Plaza Hotel's famed Oak Room. After moving to Los Angeles in 1925, he worked in a number of restaurants, learning who was important and what those important people enjoyed eating before opening his own restaurant in 1932.

The fact that Perino spared no expense in catering to his patrons was one reason for the restaurant's popularity. One waiter was assigned to every eight diners seated at tables (or at the more desirable banquettes) in the peach-colored, oval dining room. The napery was the best Irish linen money could buy, canned goods rarely appeared on the kitchen shelves, and everything from veal and fish stocks to spaghetti sauces was made on the premises.

Angelo Perino sold the place in 1969 but stayed on as a consultant to the new corporate owners for a time. Nevertheless, the spirit was gone, and despite a few futile gestures (like a line of frozen food, which Spago's Wolfgang Puck would so successfully market a couple of decades later), nothing worked.

Nobody knows what to do with the building. New zoning prohibits it from being a restaurant. Perhaps it might end up as a bank one day. Until then, it sits, a decaying container of some of Hollywood's most glamorous memories of a generation and more ago.

No story of Hollywood's lost restaurants would be complete without at least mentioning two early examples of celebrity-owned restaurants. One was the It, an effort by Clara Bow, the "It girl." The other was screenwriter and director Preston Sturges's three-level eatery complete with nightclub and barbershop, named the Players after the famous theater club on New York's Gramercy Park and located on Sunset Boulevard across from the Garden of Allah. The Players was thronged by Sturges's friends, among them Charlie Chaplin, Betty Hutton, Barbara Stanwyck, William Wyler, and the reclusive Howard Hughes. But unless you wanted to be cast in a Sturges comedy (he would often use his restaurant's patrons as extras in his urbane, witty films) or had a hankering for a little fantasizing, you could pretty well take or leave the Players and the It restaurant.

La Rue, at least during its early years of existence, was something else altogether. La Rue was founded in 1945 and co-owned for the first five years of its twenty-four years of existence by the *Hollywood Reporter's* (and Trocadero) owner Billy Wilkenson. There, seated in booth number one, upholstered like all the booths in garish gold leather, Wilkerson would hold court, gathering news items and gossip from the likes of Walt Disney and Marlene Dietrich for his trade paper. Wilkerson sold the restaurant to his partners in 1950, and they ran it for another nineteen years before closing in 1969.

For Hollywood old-timers, it's also impossible to forget Don the Beachcomber. It was the first of the tropical-themed restaurants that later sprang up across America and, in many ways, was the best. Small and virtually impossible to find (unless you knew where you were going) in a nondescript building originally erected as a duplex apartment, the restaurant soared to the top of the pantheon of celebrated saloons when Ernest Beaumont-Gantt, the Beachcomber himself, invented and popularized that most lethal of rum drinks, the Zombie. He and his wife, Cora, also created the far more benign rumaki, the bacon-wrapped chicken liver and water chestnut appetizer that became a cliché of 1950s and '60s entertaining.

In the tiny restaurant's even tinier dining rooms, each with a theme name ("the Black Hole of Calcutta" was one), sarong-clad waitresses served stars like Bing Crosby, Marlene Dietrich, and many more, all of whose chopsticks, used to enjoy the bastardized South Seas and Cantonese cuisine, were publicly displayed in a glass case. And a rain machine would periodically shower the corrugated tin roof with a tropical rainstorm. A bit tacky? Certainly. But Hollywood loved it. And still misses it.

And finally, more famous than all of the above in its day, there was Schwab's drugstore. Much of its fame arose from the legend that Lana Turner had been discovered while sitting at its counter sipping a soda. The story made Schwab's a gathering place for the hopefuls as well as the general store—as most drugstores were in the 1930s and '40s—of the stars.

The truth was that Turner (whose real first name was Judy, not Lana) was indeed discovered sitting at a drugstore counter in 1935 by the aforementioned Billy Wilkerson. But it was probably at Curries's Soda Shop, across the street from Hollywood High School where she was a student (another story says it was at the neighboring Top Hat Soda

Shop), not at Schwab's. Nevertheless, Schwab's, founded the same year as Turner's discovery by a family that owned six pharmacies around town, became so popular with the film crowd that it was nicknamed "Schwabadero," after Wilkerson's popular Trocadero supper club.

As more than one writer observed, Schwab's was the great social leveler for a generation. Seated at its counter, at the corner of Sunset Boulevard and Crescent Heights, across the street from the Garden of Allah and Preston Sturges's Players restaurant-cum-nightclub, one could spot just about every star in town, from Chaplin and Orson Welles in the 1930s right through to Judy Garland and Marilyn Monroe in the 1950s.

And they weren't there just to buy aspirin or Alka-Seltzer, either. The lunch (and dinner) counter served up memorable offerings ranging from the industry standard weekend breakfast of lox and bagels to steak and fried chicken. Columnist Sidney Skolsky decided it was the best place in town to gather gossip and moved into an office on the second floor, overlooking all the action. In 1954, part of that action included James Dean and Natalie Wood breakfasting at the counter, running their lines for *Rebel Without a Cause*. Wood, seventeen, then having an affair with the film's director, Nicholas Ray, would shortly begin a relationship with Dean—serious grist for any gossip columnist's mill.

Women stars, hopefuls, and homemakers bought their cosmetics there; on one memorable occasion Marlene Dietrich, stocking up on her favorite shade of lipstick, actually waited on an unsuspecting customer. Young and out-of-work actors and actresses, like Lucille Ball, were often "comped," and stars-to-be, like Ava Gardner and Hugh O'Brien, started their rise to fame behind the counter at Schwab's, making the drugstore's famed chocolate sodas. The place was open through the night, and prescriptions as well as anything else one might need would be delivered across the street to residents of the Garden of Allah as well as to Malibu, thirty miles away, which was quickly becoming the weekend hideaway of the stars.

Schwab's lasted until 1988, when it was replaced by an upscale mall. Where Clark Gable used to eat scrambled eggs and onions, the hoi polloi now consume Wolfgang Puck's pizzas; where Mickey Rooney and Groucho Marx and, a little later, Ronald Reagan sipped coffee and talked movie gossip, kids buy CDs at a superstore.

When Schwab's died, no Joni Mitchell sang a good-bye as she did for the Garden of Allah across the street. But today, few members of the film industry who were around in those days can talk about Schwab's drugstore without a sigh.

Spencer Tracy was only one of hundreds of Hollywood stars, including Marlene Dietrich, Judy Garland, Mickey Rooney, and Betty Grable, who turned out to serve coffee and cake, wash dishes, and occasionally entertain up to three thousand servicemen every night at the Hollywood Canteen. When the place opened in October 1942, the crowd was so large, that Bette Davis, president of the Canteen, had to crawl through a window to get in.

Nine Million Cups of Coffee—
Hollywood Goes to War

The biggest event of the twentieth century as far as the film capital was concerned was World War II. Not only did many of its male stars march off to fight the Axis (and female stars follow to entertain the troops), but for many of the studios the war changed the content of film itself.

The war—and the way the stars fought it—also changed the attitudes of millions of film fans toward the stars. Actors are frequently portrayed as above the fray that embroils the lives of their fans. But for a few years, Hollywood had its own memorial to the war, which was also a memorial to the essential good-heartedness and generosity of hundreds of actors, however much they were paid and adulated: the Hollywood Canteen. Today the sound of musicians like Harry James playing the big band hits of the time at the Canteen echo only in the memories of the few who still remember. But in its time, the Hollywood Canteen, in addition to the tremendous morale-lifting job it did, brought hundreds of stars down from their firmament and a little closer to their fans.

Today, six decades after the war, and with the little silk window flags bearing a simple star commemorating so many families' sacrifices now moldering in the bottom of drawers or lost in attics (a blue star signified a son, brother, or father in the service; a gold star memorialized one killed or lost in action), it's easy to forget the conflict. But although none of America's cities were ever touched with the horrors that fell upon Tokyo, Dresden, Rotterdam, London, Shanghai, and finally Hiroshima and Nagaski, everything we did or thought was affected by it. And much of that impact was created by films from Hollywood.

No longer were the brittle, sophisticated comedies from Paramount in vogue or the Hallmark greeting card platitudes of MGM or the dark social dramas of Warner Brothers. The movies went to war along with the boys.

Although the war finally ended the Great Depression (during which much of Hollywood's escapist product generally prospered), it also created the industry's first money problems. Foreign sales of Hollywood's films dried up overnight, and it would be years before that market returned. Many actors were forced to take salary cuts, and budgets were slashed. There was one compensation, however. Replacing expensive backgrounds in pictures with deep shadows in combination with stories that focused on people in desperate situations gave birth to an entire new genre of movies. The French would later dub it film noir.

Much of the rest of the product changed dramatically too, to what may best be described as "Mom and apple pie." As one commentator recalled, in movies "white picket fences replaced the grapes of wrath." This was understandable; with so many loved ones placed in harm's way, no one had the luxury to worry about much else. So as far as moviemakers and their fans were concerned, there were no social problems, there were no economic problems, and, although there was a war raging, we were on the side of the right. And actually, we were.

At home, Bing Crosby soothed concerns in Paramount musicals including *Holiday Inn* (1942), where he sentimentally sang a nation into dreaming of a *White Christmas*. Bob Hope took the nation on the *Road to Morocco* the same year, and in 1945 on the *Road to Utopia*. "Pin-up" posters of curvaceous stars (especially Betty Grable, the most famous of the pin-ups) tantalizingly reminded soldiers, sailors, marines, and flyers of what else they were missing on those ships, in those planes, and in the foxholes.

Patriotism was *the* supreme virtue, and actors, including James Stewart (who was already a flyer), Clark Gable, and Tyrone Power, went off to fight. Great directors like John Ford made propaganda films. Actors Like Lew Ayres, who starred in the great antiwar movie *All Quiet on the Western Front* in 1933, had made fifty-three films before he declared himself a conscientious objector in 1942; after that he made only three. Charlie Chaplin, despite his 1936 satire of Hitler in *The Great Dictator,* was then and long after thought of as a Communist sympathizer (however, because we shared a common enemy, Russia was then an ally despite its political system; it became a serious problem for Chaplin only after the Cold War began). It was simple: Hitler, Mussolini, and Hirohito were the enemies, and you were either for them or against them.

The entertainment industry turned out in force to help with the war effort; it is estimated that nearly a quarter of a million people, from celebrities to the lowest level employees in associated industries, sold war bonds and solicited blood donations. Bob Hope was probably the most visible and the best remembered for his tireless travels entertaining the troops, but no less remarkable was the time and energy given by scores of such superstars as Bing Crosby, Dorothy Lamour, and Lana Turner. Turner once sold a $5,000 war bond to a young man in Portland, Oregon, for a kiss. Ginger Rogers, who with Fred Astaire made up the most popular dancing couple of the 1930s, sold a pair of her dancing shoes for $50,000 to help the war effort. Veronica Lake auctioned off a lock of hair from her famous swoopy hairdo for $185,000.

A majority of the servicemen who fought in the Pacific were shipped off to the war through Los Angeles, and at the time it seemed that all of them wanted to see Hollywood as much as the film industry wanted to display its patriotism.

Apparently it was the actor John Garfield, who later costarred in *Gentlemen's Agreement,* Hollywood's 1948 indictment of anti-Semitism, who came up with the idea of organizing the Hollywood Canteen. The canteen would be a place where the boys could meet celebrated female stars—among them Marlene Dietrich—who in turn could show the world that they were just like anybody else as they served up coffee and doughnuts to the boys. Male stars not in uniform were welcome to help also. Andy Hardy and Mickey Rooney (before he went off to war in 1944) would occasionally play the drums in the band.

Garfield also had the brilliant idea of drafting Bette Davis, then nearing the height of her fame from her starring roles in *The Little Foxes* and *The Man Who Came to Dinner* (both released in 1941), to be the Canteen's president. She immediately discovered and rented a former livery stable and little theater at 1451 Cahuenga Boulevard, only a couple of blocks from the historic center of Hollywood, for a hundred dollars a month. (It was later replaced with a parking structure.) Like charity leaders before and since, she knew how to strong-arm people to get what she wanted. Not only did she talk the unions into allowing hundreds of studio workmen to completely remodel the old barn, she also convinced Jules Stein, the president of her agency, MCA, to help. And help he did.

For the canteen's gala opening night in October 1942, Stein (who was much later to become a humanitarian legend in Hollywood with his endowment of the Jules Stein Eye Clinic) organized a benefit that raised thousands of dollars (ten thousand dollars alone from the sale of bleacher seats to the show). Eddie Cantor was master of ceremonies, Bud Abbott and Lou Costello entertained, and four bands played, including the heartthrob of the era, Rudy Vallee; the Coast Guard Band; Kay Kyser and his band; Duke Ellington; and the U.S. Army Air Force Band from the Santa Ana Air Base. The place—decorated with Western murals painted by film cartoonists and nationally famous artists—was so crowded with servicemen, Davis later recalled that she had to crawl through a window to get in. Soon after, Harry Cohn, the crusty head of Columbia Pictures, gave the canteen sixty-five hundred dollars from a benefit premiere of *Talk of the Town,* a film that starred Ronald Coleman, Jean Arthur, and Cary Grant. He also persuaded Davis's studio, Warners, to make a film called *Hollywood Canteen* in 1943 (released in 1944), which starred the actress, and part of the film's gross went to support the club.

Davis devoted hours to getting other stars to help, once famously asking the Austrian-born Hedy Lamarr to help out in the kitchen. "I couldn't cook," Lamarr said later. "I was a mess in the kitchen. I would wash dishes gladly." And for two nights a week that's just what she did to support the war effort of her adopted homeland. Coincidentally, that's where she met her third husband, actor John Loder, who was drying dishes.

Many of the stars joined the volunteer hostesses in jitterbugging with the GIs below the chandeliers made from old wagon wheels and kerosene lamps converted to electricity. Betty Grable met her husband, Harry James, while he was conducting his band at the Canteen. Greer Garson, Carole Landis, and Olivia de Havilland were just a few of the many stars who joined the thirty-five hundred hostesses, who were not allowed to reveal their last names, phone numbers, or addresses to the servicemen (nor were they—officially—allowed to date them). Marlene Dietrich did everything from dancing with the GIs to washing dishes to serving at the snack bar. Busboys included Fred MacMurray, Basil Rathbone, George Murphy, John Garfield, Louis Calhern, and the great French actor Jean Gabin.

Eventually nearly every star in Hollywood signed up to help. Entertainers included Edgar Bergen (with his puppet sidekick, Charlie Mc Carthy), Red Skelton, and Dinah Shore. Secretaries from the studios were even on hand to take dictation for letters home.

There was a downside, of course. Actress Gene Tierney, a spectacular beauty, contracted German measles while working at the Canteen when she was twenty-two and pregnant; as a result her daughter (with Paramount costume designer and Russian aristocrat Oleg Cassini) was born retarded. Years afterward, Tierney met a woman at a tennis party in Los Angeles who asked her if she had caught measles after the two had met at the Hollywood Canteen. The woman went on to explain that she had been stationed at a nearby Marine Corps camp that had been swept with an epidemic of the measles and had deliberately broken quarantine to meet her favorite star at the Hollywood Canteen—Gene Tierney. Although Tierney made many more films (most notably *The Razor's Edge* in 1946), she was never the same afterward, attempted suicide several times, and before her return to films in *Advise and Consent* (1962) was committed to a mental institution. In the best tradition of Hollywood cannibalizing its own, her tragedy then served as the fictionalized basis of several films.

Over the years, more than six thousand stars and industry talent (including writers and directors) signed up to host, cook, do dishes, and clean up. Admission was by uniform, and although the capacity of the Hollywood Canteen was limited by the fire department to no more than five hundred, some three thousand men per night (nearly a hundred thousand a month) was the average. Everything was free, including cigarettes, milk, coffee, sandwiches, and cake. It was once estimated that the value of the music provided by two bands nightly, if purchased, was somewhere around a million dollars a year.

Sharing a similar name, "Mom" Lehr's Hollywood Guild and Canteen on North Crescent Heights Boulevard (not far from the Garden of Allah) did its part for the war effort by housing and serving three meals a day to up to twelve hundred servicemen in Hollywood on forty-eight-hour passes. Such an operation was expensive and drew on the fund-raising talents of Mary Pickford, Janet Gaynor, and Myrna Loy and the generosity of the Hollywood Canteen itself, which contributed fifty-two thousand dollars annually to the Hollywood Guild's support.

The day the war ended, August 14, 1945, Hollywood, like the rest of the nation, went wild. Traffic was brought to a standstill as people danced in the street amid a downpour of confetti. That night the intersection of Hollywood and Vine, then the film capital's equivalent of New York's Time Square, was impassable. Nearby, more than three thousand servicemen and women again jammed the Hollywood Canteen to celebrate.

Three months later it was all over. The Hollywood Canteen, its work done, closed its doors on November 22. Bob Hope and Jack Benny led the host of mourners who bid it farewell. It had been open every day for three years, one month, and twenty-eight days. In that time it fed and entertained nearly four million servicemen, giving out nearly three million packs of cigarettes, six million pieces of cake, 125,000 gallons of milk, and nine million cups of coffee.

"Above and beyond the call of duty" is a famous military citation. It certainly applied to the work of the Hollywood Canteen and the thousands of volunteers who made it happen.

The Lamps of Hollywood—Decay and Rebirth of the Capital of Dreams

On the eve of World War I, Edward, Viscount Grey of Fallodon, uttered a line that, pessimistic as it sounded, helped galvanize the Allied powers to meet the forthcoming struggle. "The lamps are going out all over Europe," he said; "we shall not see them lit again in our lifetime." Happily, he was wrong; although millions tragically died in the subsequent slaughter, the lamps eventually went back on—at least until World War II again extinguished them for a time.

During the 1960s, '70s, and '80s, you could have said much the same of Hollywood. Beset by the popularity of television, the government-forced breakup of the studio-exhibitor monopoly (which kept the studios in business), and the rising popularity of independent filmmaking, not to mention the free-agentry practiced by celebrity actors with the collapse of the contract system, the lamps of Hollywood were going out all over town as residents fled both middle- and upper-class neighborhoods for the San Fernando Valley and the safer, less crowded Westside of Los Angeles.

Businesses, from the filmmakers to the service industries to the small shops along Hollywood Boulevard, simply vanished, to be replaced by sleazy mini-malls, tattoo parlors, and cheap souvenir shops catering to the few tourists who would forsake Disneyland to visit a town whose once-glittering tinsel was rusting. Drugs arrived in force— among the most famous crack houses was the apartment building where Carol Burnett was raised. And gangs, too. By the late 1980s, the problem had become so bad that those few residents who remained in once-celebrated buildings like the El Cabrillo, built by Cecil B. De-Mille in 1927, would often have to lie on the floor to avoid being hit by bullets flying through their windows.

Hollywood's survival, as both a physical entity and a metaphor, would in many ways also resemble a war, and a long one. But eventually those lamps started going on again in the film capital. Firm police presence and action began to control the drug and gang problems; new, younger residents, attracted by the romance of Hollywood and the low rents, started returning. Businesses too. Disney completed a stunning restoration of the El Capitan Theater, one of the showcase movie houses from film's Golden Age. The legendary Egyptian Theater, where in the silent era, films by such stars as Douglas Fairbanks, Mary Pickford, Ramon Novarro, and Lillian Gish were premiered, was restored as the permanent home of the American Film Institute. The Academy of Motion Picture Arts and Sciences announced that by 2002 Oscar would have a permanent home in a new, multimillion-dollar theater to be built at the corner of Hollywood Boulevard and Highland Avenue, site of the old Hollywood Hotel. By the end of the 1990s, half a billion dollars had been committed for remodeling Hollywood.

But something seemed missing.

In 1922, Earle C. Anthony, whose Packard dealership provided many of the now-legendary cars for stars of the silent and early sound era, discovered a new kind of electric sign while vacationing in Paris. It wasn't illuminated by dozens, hundreds, or (as in the case of the Hollywood sign erected two years later) thousands of electric light bulbs but by a glass tube filled with argon gas, which glowed with brilliant color when an electric current was passed through it. Anthony was so enchanted with the possibilities of the new lighting, called neon, that he ordered three blue-and-orange signs in the then-familiar Packard logo script for his dealership, two of which he mounted on the roof of his showroom. They were almost certainly the first neon signs anywhere in America.

In no time Los Angeles became the twentieth century's City of Neon, with thousands of signs creating avenues of light through the sultry nights. Writers, including William Faulkner, Christopher Isherwood, and John O'Hara, were entranced with the result—Los Angeles as Oz—and many used the galaxy of neon as a metaphor for the film capital itself.

To F. Scott Fitzgerald the signs also conveyed the schizophrenia of the place: creating fantasy while anchored in fact, conjuring escapist dreams amid worldwide economic depression, cold-blooded corruption alongside sentimental innocence. LA's noir novelist, Raymond Chandler, even wrote an ode to the city's neon in his mystery novel *The Little Sister*. "I smelled Los Angeles before I got to it," he wrote, "it smelled stale and old like a living room that has been closed too long. But the colored lights fooled you. The lights were wonderful. There ought to be a monument to the man who invented neon lights."

In 1942, Los Angeles mayor Fletcher Brown ordered the lights blacked out amid rumors of a possible Japanese air raid on the city. (In fact, LA's civil defense headquarters were in MacArthur Park, by then literally encircled by bright neon signs.) It would be some fifty years before they came on again.

Inspired by Chandler's novel, the general manager of the city's Cultural Affairs Department, Cuban-born Adolfo Nodal, decided to do what he could to restore the signs, both for their metaphoric resonance and as a morale booster and visual antidote to the decay of many historic neighborhoods. It took a lot of time, energy, and money, but it worked—spectacularly—as is clear to anyone who walks the streets of Hollywood or the Wilshire Center area today. Los Angeles is once again host to one of the greatest displays of neon in the world.

Altogether, 125 gigantic display signs were reborn in Hollywood and along the Wilshire corridor. Some signs were even discovered to contain traces of their original gas when the restorers went to work. Many of them—like the signs again atop the Egyptian, Pacific, and Pantages Theaters, the Hollywood Roosevelt Hotel, the Hotel Knickerbocker, and apartments like the El Royal and Mae West's Ravenswood—evoke again the brassy glamour of a Lost Hollywood as they glow in the night.

Hollywood, the Dream Capital of the world, was reborn. You had only to look up in the sky to know it.

The lamps were on again.

Index